BROWNS
GLORY

D1372636

BROWNS GLORY

FOR THE LOVE OF OZZIE, THE TOE, AND OTTO

ALAN ROSS

Cumberland House
Nashville, Tennessee

Copyright © 2005 by Alan Ross

Published by
Cumberland House Publishing, Inc.
431 Harding Industrial Drive
Nashville, TN 37211–3160

All rights reserved. No part of this book may be reproduced or transmitted in any form or by any means, electronic or mechanical, including photocopying and recording, or by any information storage and retrieval system, without permission in writing from the publisher, except for brief quotations in critical reviews and articles.

Cover design: Gore Studio, Inc., Nashville, Tennessee
Book design: John Mitchell
Research assistant: Andrew Gearing Ross
Special thanks to Dino Lucarelli, Cleveland Browns alumni relations manager, for photo and roster assistance

Library of Congress Cataloging-in-Publication Data
Ross, Alan, 1944–
  Browns glory : for the love of Ozzie, the Toe, and Otto / Alan Ross.
     p. cm.
  Includes bibliographical references and index.
  ISBN 1-58182-448-3 (pbk. : alk. paper)
  1. Cleveland Browns (Football team : 1946-1995)—History.
I. Title.
  GV956.C6R65 2005
  796.332'64'0977132—dc22

                                                      2005015908

Printed in Canada

1 2 3 4 5 6 7—11 10 09 08 07 06 05

For Duey Graham,
your friendship is a prized gift,
Ottomatically

and for Caroline,
thank you, darling, for your
tireless support, loyalty, and most of all,
deeply devoted love

Otto Graham

Photo Courtesy of the Cleveland Browns

CONTENTS

INTRODUCTION

It was my first trip to historic Cleveland Municipal Stadium. The dilapidated steel-and-concrete fortress stood massively against a gray sky, snow falling lightly, on Dec. 15, 1991. Reverence seems to surround old relics. Honor comes easily to antiquity.

I wandered the ground-level concourse, neck craned upward, before spotting the stylish wainscoting still in evidence underneath the mezzanine overhang, a decorative element not to be found at Jacobs Field or the new Cleveland Browns Stadium. The wraiths of previous Browns glory exuded from every pore of the ancient building: the specters of leather-helmeted Otto Graham, Lou Groza, Horace Gillom, Marion Motley, Mac Speedie, and Dante Lavelli; the sleek, explosive bursts of Jim Brown, Bobby Mitchell, and Paul Warfield; the string of mini-miracles provided by Brian Sipe and the Kardiac Kids.

Now here I was, watching the 1990s Brown-and-Orange edition tackle their bedeviling Central Division rivals from Houston. As Warren Moon passed the Oilers into a 17–14 lead deep in the fourth quarter, a sinking doom permeated the faithful. Reflecting the Browns' powerlessness on the field, radio reports brayed of treacherous roads around Cleveland, slick from mounting ice and snow.

The game wound down. But then quarterback Bernie Kosar began to untrack his team, a final drive underway. With untypical agility on the slippery surface, Kosar danced from the Oilers' 23 all the way down to the 2. The old stadium erupted in a thunderous roar, and I wondered if the old wainscoting would split and splinter under the strain of the tumult.

Time for one last play. Browns kicker Matt Stover lined up on the 9-yard line for the chip-shot field goal that would send the game into overtime. At last, I was getting the payoff for what I had driven 525 miles to see: a real football game, in the cold north, outdoors, in snow! The snap, the hold, the kick. *Doink.* Stover bricked a line-drive squibber left of the uprights that never reached the height of the crossbar. Silently, 55,680 frozen witnesses began their death-march file to the exits. A freewheeling, 360-degree spin on icy I-71 South was the lone excitement on the long, eight-hour drive back.

As I began to assemble *Browns Glory*—the story of the Cleveland Browns, as told through the players, coaches, assistants, owners, opponents, fans, and members of the media — the recollection of that day at Municipal Stadium brought on a smile. Over the years, Browns victories have been plentiful but the number of lasting memories even more so.

So, don your Browns game jersey and grab your dawg bone. You're headed for pure unadulterated Turkey and The Toe; Diek and Dub; Shaf and The Sheik; Gunner and Glue Fingers; Dopey, Smokey, and Minnie . . . and Special Delivery.

It's all Browns.

REMEMBRANCE

IT WAS THE SUNDAY of Thanksgiving weekend, 1954. November 28, to be exact. Coming out of church, my father, after conferring with a friend, casually asked me, "How'd you like to go see the Cleveland Browns today?" This was like asking Babe Ruth if he'd like a chili dog. Such a question needed no reply, as if, in my breathless state, I could have given one.

This dream-like bonanza came with additional gold lining: I was actually going to get to see Otto Graham. The Browns master quarterback was my first pro football hero, and it wasn't every day a kid got to witness his idol in action — especially in the 1950s when TV appearances by any NFL team were rare.

Two hours later we were at the Polo Grounds, the New York Giants' venerable venue in Harlem. Our seats were perched high in the curving upper grandstand in left-center field. Configured for football, it translated to a bird's eye view above the right-hand corner of one of the end zones.

Of course, the magnificent Graham was his usual brilliant self, passing and running with the effortless athleticism that made him a future Hall of Famer and one of the sport's iconic legends. Specifically, though it was 50 years ago, I remember him evading a fierce pass rush with graceful ease, barely escaping at arm's length from sure disaster, rolling right somewhere around the Giants' 25-yard line before firing a bullet to receiver Darrel Brewster on a sideline route at the 2.

But it was another play, still standing out with vivid clarity, that turned out to be one for the ages. Punter Horace Gillom stood on his own 5-yard line, his back to us, and launched a gargantuan shot that seemed to pierce the dull winter sky overhead. I remember hearing the entire stadium "ooh" in jaw-dropping awe, as Gillom's punt soared towards the heavens. I looked down to see the Giants safety turn his back to the play and run with all his might toward his own goal line, the punt having rocketed over his head by some 20 yards. After what seemed an eternity, the ball finally hit the ground and rolled the remaining 10 yards into the New York end zone for a touchback. Yes, it was Gillom's stratospheric 80-yard punt that can still be found in the club's records as the longest punt in Cleveland Browns history. In all, from the point where the ball touched Gillom's foot, the kick traveled 95 yards.

I was eternally hooked, babbling incessantly about the game for weeks afterward. I doubt my father, who wasn't into sports, ever really knew how much his generous, kind act meant to a 10-year-old kid with budding Brown and Orange in his heart.

— A.R.

BROWNS
TRADITION

THE BROWNS WERE A blue-collar team with no logo, and Cleveland is the cradle of football. Football was almost invented here.

Jerry Sherk
defensive tackle (1970–81)

Arch, I'm not here for a social call. I understand you're starting a new professional football league. I'd like to get a franchise for Cleveland.

Mickey McBride

first Cleveland Browns owner (1946–53),
to Arch Ward, Chicago Tribune sports editor and College All-Star Game founder, who was putting together a new professional football league for 1946—the All-America Football Conference, of which the Browns would be admitted as a charter member

Paul was the easiest person I ever hired. I could have signed him for $15,000, but I wanted to make a big splash for publicity so I gave him $25,000. I wanted to say my team had the highest paid coach in America.

Mickey McBride

on the hiring of Paul Brown as the Cleveland Browns' first head coach, Feb. 8, 1945

Joe Louis was the best-known champion at the time, and we received a lot of entries suggesting we name the team the Brown Bombers. So we decided to shorten the name and call the team the Browns.

Paul Brown
head coach (1946–62)

According to author Jack Clary, "One of Mickey McBride's promotions allowed the fans to select a name for his new team. The winning selection: the Cleveland Panthers. But the name Panthers already had prior ownership—it was the name of a semi-pro team near Cleveland—and worse, Paul Brown discovered that the team had been a chronic loser. So McBride staged another contest, with the trend shifting toward naming the team after champions."

Not a single entry in the contest listed Louis or his nickname as a reason for choosing "Browns."

Zac Jackson
*editor/writer,
ClevelandBrowns.com*

The Browns' seal-brown and burnt-orange uniform colors were adapted by Paul Brown from Bowling Green State University's color scheme.

Steve Byrne
author

BGSU was the site of the Browns' training camp from 1946 to 1951.

The foundation of the team was being hand-picked, as an art connoisseur would select from among the world's art treasures.

Jack Clary

author

Most of the original Browns were fairly well-known commodities to Paul Brown: returning servicemen and players that Brown either had coached or coached against while at Ohio State or, during World War II, at Great Lakes Naval Station.

He beat my Ohio State teams two of the three games we played against Northwestern. That spoke well enough of his ability, but he also had other qualities. He could throw as well running to his right as he could running to his left. He had great peripheral vision from being a great basketball player, and the more I thought about him, the more I considered him the ultimate.

Paul Brown

on quarterback Otto Graham, the first player signed by the Cleveland Browns

Marion Motley made his professional football debut with the Browns in 1946, joining teammate Bill Willis as the first blacks in the pro game since the early 1930s. Although they endured untold hardships and bigotry in the months preceding the 1947 baseball debut of Jackie Robinson, they never received equal credit for their social breakthroughs.

Ron Smith
author

The stadium wasn't the best thing going, but there was just a lot of tradition that lived there.

Galen Fiss
linebacker (1956–66)

It was not a smell, it was an aroma. You could smell the mustard in the concourses, and it made you want a hot dog.

David Dwoskin
on the unique scent permeating Municipal Stadium in the 1950s. Dwoskin later bought the rights to "Stadium Mustard" and now markets it worldwide

When the Browns started winning in the old AAFC, people really got into football. The Cleveland Rams never caught on. But after the war, Paul Brown got a lot of Ohio State players, and that helped. When you start winning automatically, it really forms a terrific relationship. Then they beat the Eagles in 1950 and contended for the championship six of the next seven years. That cemented the tradition.

Greg Brinda
Cleveland sports talk show host

From 1946 through 1971, only once did the Cleveland Browns endure a season where there were more losses than victories. No other team can make such a claim.

Jack Clary

An intense man who can rarely be found at ease. He is static tension, three packs of half-smoked cigarettes, and a peripatetic schedule.

The Plain Dealer
on Art Modell

I grew up in Warren, Ohio, watching the Browns on TV. When I came to the team in 1964, I felt I had to prove I was worthy to wear their colors.

Paul Warfield
*Hall of Fame wide receiver
(1964–69, 1976–77)*

Former coach Nick Skorich would tell the players that the city would rise or fall Monday based on Sunday's result.

John Keim
author

All of a sudden on a September afternoon, in 1978, I come through that tunnel and I'm the head coach of the Cleveland Browns. And I'm thinking about Dante Lavelli and Lou Groza and Otto Graham and Marion Motley and all those great players....I thought to myself, "Here I am in this place that was built in 1931." All the time I was there, that was on my mind every single time I went on that field.

Sam Rutigliano
head coach (1978–84)

The Kardiac Kids gave all those people something to hold onto. It seemed like the entire community thoroughly engulfed the Browns. That year, the team and the city were one.

Thom Darden
safety (1972–74, 1976–81),
on the 1979–80 Browns

I want to play in Cleveland.

Bernie Kosar
*quarterback (1985–1993),
before the 1985 supplemental
draft*

Quarterback Bernie Kosar, a Youngstown native, became an icon in the 1980s when he declared his desire to return to northern Ohio and play for the Browns, after leading the University of Miami to a national title. After guiding the Browns into three AFC championship games, Kosar's popularity skyrocketed. It was unmatched by anyone in the city. Maybe even the state.

John Keim

The cause of their rage was obvious. Art Modell was deemed a traitor to Cleveland and its people. For years the fans had supported the Browns with sellout crowds and intense loyalty, even though their beloved team had never rewarded that devotion with a trip to the Super Bowl. Modell had promised he would never move the Browns, but now he had done so. Clevelanders were seeing their historic and envied support of the Browns rewarded with treachery. Modell said he made the decision to move because he "had no choice." The fans did not believe him. To them, Art Modell was a deceitful villain. Pure and simple.

Michael Poplar

author

I'm so positive of Bill Belichick's future here, and that of the Cleveland Browns organization, that if we don't get the job done by the end of his contract [1995], I will get out of football and leave Cleveland.

Art Modell
Dec. 30, 1992

If Bill won five Super Bowls in a row in Cleveland, they would still never accept him because he cut Bernie Kosar.

Steve Belichick
*father of former
head coach Bill Belichick*

A Prince Charming entered his life, and Prince Baltimore brought with him a golden stadium opportunity, shining with significant new revenue possibilities. Modell had to seriously consider a divorce. He knew he would have to act fast, or the gift-laden Prince would disappear forever.

Michael Poplar

The Cleveland Browns are part of the fabric of the people of northeast Ohio. Anyone tells you anything different, they're wrong. This was their team. Modell didn't own it. They invested their time, their money, their feelings. These were the best fans in the world.

Jim Kanicki
defensive tackle (1963–69)

The Cleveland Browns have one of the most storied and fascinating histories and backgrounds of any team in the NFL. We have heroes. We even have villains. This community is so wedded to the concept of the Browns, it's right up there with family and religion.

Carmen Policy
president/chief executive officer (1999–2003)

In an unprecedented move, the NFL guaranteed Cleveland a team by 1999. The colors and nickname remained, while the old franchise became the Baltimore Ravens.

John Keim

Browns teams used to be the ones to beat. They earned that regard over the years. There has been a winning tradition here. . . . We are out to regain that old prestige. We start with horizons unlimited. A unique joy and ecstasy comes from winning. We must win.

Nick Skorich

*head coach (1971–74)/
assistant coach (1964–70)*

My happiest days were coaching the Browns.

Blanton Collier

head coach (1963–70),
who, in addition to serving 11
years as an assistant under Paul
Brown at Cleveland, was also
head coach at Kentucky
(1954–61)

I have to admit, my heart belongs to the Cleveland Browns.

Paul Warfield

We didn't sit around the locker room talking about Paul Brown or Jim Brown. We were too busy trying to make legends out of ourselves. But in our private moments, most of us thought about the tradition.

Jerry Sherk

We're not an expansion team. We're the Cleveland Browns.

Carmen Policy

on the return of the Browns in
1999

THE BROWN AND ORANGE

FIFTEEN PLAYERS WHO WORE the Brown and Orange and one legendary coach who orchestrated them have been honored in that exclusive fraternity that resides in Canton, Ohio. And while the immortal Browns—Graham, Motley, Willis, Brown, Groza, Warfield, and the rest—produced enough lasting memories for enshrinement in bronze, the toiling of the merely mortal day-to-day players who generated far less press dot the prolific landscape that is Cleveland Browns football. A few may still gain a Hall of Fame nod one day, but like the blue-collar pride that permeates the great city by the lake, these players executed their tasks in true blue-collar fashion, integral cogs all.

Mac Speedie was fast, but he made so much use of his slow-fast-slow technique that no one realized just how much speed he really had. He was an instinctive, deceptive receiver and so tall that, when running at top speed, he seemed to be gliding easily. That's why so many defensive backs were fooled by his running style. If I played against him, I might well have considered guarding him with three men in some combination.

Paul Brown

on the underrated Browns end (1946–52)

Mac Speedie should be in the Hall of Fame with Lavelli. I covered the guy every day in practice, and I never saw a better receiver than Speedie.

Tommy James

cornerback (1948–55)

Tommy James was one of the great defensive backs, but nobody wrote about him. The year the Rams beat us for the championship [24–17 in 1951], Tom Fears caught two long touchdown passes. Tommy James got blamed for that, and it was damned Cliff Lewis's fault. The pictures showed Tommy James chasing Tom Fears, and it wasn't even his man. He's one of those guys that people overlooked all the time, but that guy belongs in the Hall of Fame.

Tony Adamle
linebacker (1947–51, 1954)

George Young was 10 times the football player Len Ford was.

Tony Adamle
*on the Browns' defensive end
who played from 1946 through
1953*

Tony Adamle was as intelligent a player as I ever had, but he was also tough inside. There was never a player or a team that Adamle feared, and when he went after someone, he really went after him.

Paul Brown

on the former Browns captain

I wanted him with Lavelli and Speedie because he was the third dimension for our passing game. He had so many moves it was almost impossible for him not to get open and impossible, also, for any team to cover him with just one man.

Paul Brown

on halfback/receiver Dub Jones

Long before Ray Guy, he was known for focusing on what we now call "hang time."

Ace Davis

BerniesInsiders.com,
on punter Horace Gillom
(1947–56)

PHOTO COURTESY OF THE CLEVELAND BROWNS

Horace Gillom

Horace Gillom might have broken Sammy Baugh's punting record if he'd kicked strictly for distance.

Bob Carroll

Pro Football Researchers Association

I thought Milt Plum was the perfect quarterback for Paul Brown. I always thought Milt Plum was going to be there forever. Milt listened to Paul. Mechanically, he was excellent. When Milt left, it was unbelievable, because you had a guy who didn't make very many mistakes. He was a Paul Brown-type quarterback.

Dick Schafrath

left tackle (1959–71)

Plum was traded to Detroit before the 1962 season, after published remarks critical of Paul Brown's play-calling, in particular Brown's refusal to let his QBs change plays at the line of scrimmage.

I liked to hit people.

Bob Gain

defensive tackle (1952, 1954–64)

Paul Brown was in love with a runner named Ernie Davis, who had just broken all of Jim Brown's rushing records at Syracuse. The Washington Redskins were looking for a player to break their color line [Washington had no black players until 1962], and the Redskins knew that Bobby Mitchell was classy and bright, the perfect guy to do it. So the Browns traded Mitchell and a No. 1 pick to Washington for the draft rights to Syracuse star Ernie Davis.

Terry Pluto

Ernie Davis was diagnosed with leukemia just as training camp opened. Modell believed that Davis deserved a chance to play in a game, almost as a dying wish. Davis also had been cleared by one doctor to play.

Terry Pluto

Paul Brown refused to [play Ernie Davis]. They finally compromised by putting the poor kid in a uniform, introducing him before a game, and having him run across the field in a spotlight.

Hal Lebovitz

longtime Cleveland sports journalist with The Plain Dealer *and* News-Herald, *on Ernie Davis*

One of the concrete disappointments from the fallout of Davis's fate was the loss of the potential big-back backfield of Jim Brown and Davis, an equally lethal combination of power and speed.

Blanton Collier is a scientific football man, a very unusual one. He has ideas and is an outstanding teacher. He rates with the best in the scientific aspects of the game.

Paul Brown

I'm not Paul Brown. I don't want to be Paul Brown. I just want to be Blanton Collier.

Blanton Collier

It wasn't easy being Ernie Green. He could run the football. He could catch the football. He had the total offensive game. But with the Browns, he had to put all that and his ego aside. He was there to block for Jim Brown.

Paul Warfield

on Jim Brown's low-profile backfield mate from 1962–65

It would have been nice if Jim Brown had said a little more about Ernie Green. But you can look back through thousands of old newspaper stories quoting Brown on everything from running the ball to race relations, and barely find a word about Green.

Terry Pluto

That Roberts is like a fox terrier running around the legs of an elephant.

Blanton Collier

on the elusiveness of punt/kick returner Walter "The Flea" Roberts (1964–66)

I got my weight up to 265. I had to beat out five guys to win the position. Lou Groza was a huge help to me. He could still play football, but his back was bothering him so much that the poor guy couldn't even get down into a three-point stance.

Dick Schafrath

on succeeding Lou Groza as starting left tackle in the early 1960s

Blanton Collier called him "The Bulldog." That's because he'd grab on to you and never let go. When he blocked, it was like a bulldog getting his teeth into you.

Monte Clark

right tackle (1963–69), on left tackle Dick Schafrath

Gary Collins ran that post pattern to perfection, and he just may be the most underrated receiver ever to play this game.

Jim Brown

*Hall of Fame running back
(1957–65)*

I was a son of a bitch in the fourth quarter. I made the big plays. I hear people say "Michael Irvin is The Man. He wants it." I say, "That's what I did." People would ask Dub Jones, "Why did you throw the ball to Collins in that crucial situation?" And Jones would say, "I ain't stupid. I'm throwing the ball to the guy who could catch it." Guess who was on the other side? An All-Pro receiver who got selected to the Hall of Fame. But everyone knew who was catching the ball.

Gary Collins

wide receiver/punter (1962–71)

He was an unparalleled pass blocker. His man would never get to the quarterback. He'd make the rest of us look bad. And he was one of the greatest downfield blockers I've ever seen. When he went out on a sweep, his man went down and stayed on the ground. By the end of his career, he was 265 pounds, and he could still run like a high school fullback.

Monte Clark

on Gene Hickerson

He hasn't been recognized for being as good as he was. Some good players never get the recognition. He was the best lineman I played with. He could go left and right, and he had a low center of gravity. He was just a good athlete.

Jim Kanicki

on defensive tackle
Walter Johnson (1965–76)

Getting Frank Ryan was one of the best trades I ever made. The more I worked with him, the more I wished we had had him a few years earlier, because we could have won big with him as our quarterback.

Paul Brown

He was highly intelligent and a good passer. He had the ability to throw the long ball and liked to throw it. Of all the passers I played with, he threw it the best. He was just bigger and stronger than others I played with.

Paul Warfield

on Frank Ryan

Lou is my grandpa, Schaf's my dad.

Doug Dieken
left tackle (1971–84),
on his predecessors at left tackle,
Groza and Schafrath. Between
them, the three men manned
the key offensive line position
in Cleveland for 37 consecutive
years

The one who was a real street fighter was Doug Dieken. I had to face him twice a year, since the Browns were in our conference. There were no holds barred; everything was on the table. He was a very tenacious competitor. He left nothing out, from clipping to holding to biting—anything. That was all part of the game to him, and that's the way I had to gear my state of mental preparation for him.

Elvin Bethea
Hall of Fame tackle,
Houston Oilers

PHOTO COURTESY OF THE CLEVELAND BROWNS

Greg Pruitt

He might have been only 195 pounds, but he thought he was 215. We called him "King." He was the guy, an unbelievable competitor. He was one of the first generation of the little scatbacks, and he was out to prove he could play in the league.

Doug Dieken

on running back Greg Pruitt

Greg Pruitt could be the best broken field runner the Browns ever had.

Chuck Heaton

author/sports journalist

He was slower than smoke off manure, but for 10 yards he was very quick. He had that great extension, and he had great hip explosion. And he was a very smart player.

Dick Modzelewski

defensive tackle (1964–66),
on defensive tackle Jerry Sherk

Brian Sipe is extremely bright and has great mental toughness. It's the same kind of toughness the Johnny Unitases and Bart Starrs and Otto Grahams had. He might be the best ever at standing in there and concentrating in the face of the rush.

Sam Rutigliano

I was impressed with him right from the beginning. I had talked to Len Dawson, Bob Griese, and Fran Tarkenton. They were similar quarterbacks. They said he will hit the open receivers. That's a very simple statement, but very, very important. When they're open, he'll throw strikes.

Sam Rutigliano

on Brian Sipe

Brian's ability to think on his feet and make plays is uncanny.

Doug Dieken

on Brian Sipe

Brian Sipe

PHOTO COURTESY OF THE CLEVELAND BROWNS

Why does a Mike Phipps fail? Why does a Brian Sipe succeed? It's from the neck up.

Sam Rutigliano

He had the ability to dominate an entire offense. He was strong enough to take on the offensive line and fast enough to catch the running backs.

Greg Pruitt

*running back (1973–81),
on linebacker Robert L. Jackson
(1978–81), the Browns' No. 1
pick in 1977, considered the
club's best defensive prospect in
15 years. Though he played four
seasons with Cleveland,
Jackson's brilliant promise was
cut short by a devastating knee
injury in summer camp of his
rookie year*

Mike Pruitt led the team in rushing from 1979 through '83, picking up 1,000-yard seasons from 1979 through '81 and 1983. He had 1,294 yards and nine TDs in 1979 and 1,184 yards and 10 TDs in 1983. In 1980, the year of the "Kardiac Kids," Pruitt led the team in rushing and receiving [63 catches].

Mark Craig
author

This was a guy who didn't accept losing. You see that in great competitors, and I saw that in him in only his second year. I was in awe of him not being in awe of the league.

Ozzie Newsome
*Hall of Fame tight end
(1978–90),
on quarterback Bernie Kosar*

He was usually awkward and clumsy and all the negatives. He seemed to be the perfect quarterback at a time when Cleveland was ugly. But he got the job done.

Tony Grossi
The Plain Dealer,
on Bernie Kosar

Bernie was the most cerebral quarterback I ever played with. He threw the softest pass. He had the best ideas of how to beat a defense. He was at his best when calling plays in the huddle and not getting them from the sideline.

Brian Brennan
wide receiver (1984–91)

PHOTO COURTESY OF THE CLEVELAND BROWNS

Bernie Kosar

He had a special quality, more so than Brian Sipe. Sipe was more of a matinee idol, and people warmed to him. But he never won a playoff game. Bernie Kosar proved some of the smartest men in football wrong.

Tony Grossi

In just his second season, Kosar led Cleveland to a 12–4 record and the AFC Central crown, hurling 17 touchdown passes and amassing 3,854 passing yards in leading them to their first playoff win in 17 years. In that 23–20 double-overtime playoff victory over the New York Jets, Kosar threw for an NFL postseason-record 489 yards that put the Browns in the AFC Championship Game against Denver.

Bernie wasn't some starry-eyed kid. He was 23 going on 33. He had a presence to him that exceeded his age.

Doug Dieken

Give him a defense and he'll find a hole. Give him a game plan and he'll improve it. Give him a wrinkle and he'll smooth it out. He knows where to throw it, when to throw it, and how to throw it. It's hard to imagine a more intelligent quarterback.

Leigh Steinberg

agent,
on Bernie Kosar

Fans did not take kindly to Bernie's benching. The controversy was the talk of the town. Over the radio airwaves and in every sports bar, the debate raged on. While some agreed with the coach about the selection of Vinny Testaverde as the new starter, the preponderance of callers favored Kosar in the battle.

Michael Poplar

He lived in outer space and spent most of his time on Mars.

> **Anonymous Browns player**
> *on linebacker Chip Banks (1982–86)*

We were the most prepared corners in the game. We spent a tremendous amount of hours preparing and would start as soon as the game ended.

> **Hanford Dixon**
> *cornerback (1981–89),*
> *on he and fellow corner*
> *Frank Minnifield*

Deep down, Hanford Dixon was so afraid of getting burned that he refused to let it happen. He played off this bravado. I appreciated him because he worked so hard in practice, and that's why his career was cut so short. He ran his legs out.

> **Clay Matthews**
> *linebacker (1978–93)*

I'm here to learn, play football, and help this team to win. I expect to win Super Bowls.

Tim Couch
quarterback (1999–2003)

3

BROWNS CHARACTER

To ME, FOOTBALL WAS not about appearing in Nike commercials or calling attention to yourself. It was about winning, about fitting into the team. If I had been immature or not serious about my profession, they never would have accepted me. And more than anything, I wanted the acceptance and respect of those players.

Paul Warfield

Repetition is learning.

Paul Brown

on practice drills

He liked offense. He liked a team that was organized. He hated sloppy football. He'd die a million deaths watching today's game.

Kay Collier-Slone

on her father, Browns head coach Blanton Collier (1963–70). Collier was also offensive back-field coach under Paul Brown (1946–53, 1962) and an assistant under Forrest Gregg (1975–76)

Paul Brown integrated pro football without uttering a single word about integration. He just went out, signed a bunch of great black athletes, and started kicking butt. That's how you do it. You don't talk about it. Paul never said one word about race.

Jim Brown

When I came to the Browns, I thought football was blood and guts. But these guys were a bunch of scientists. The first thing I did was take an IQ test for Paul Brown. Blanton had his psychocybernetics. But all this made me a better player.

Paul Wiggin
defensive end (1957–67)

Galen Fiss was a true leader. He had an honesty about him. He could talk to everybody—the white guys, the black guys, the city guys, and the farm guys.

Jim Kanicki

Going into the game, Baltimore thought they could do anything they wanted with us. During those two weeks of practice, we kept reading, "You're gonna lose, you're gonna lose." A team in that position can either go along with that and say, "Yeah, we're gonna lose, all right," or a team can pull together and show the world how wrong it can be. We got tired of hearing it and simply said, "We're gonna win this damn game and shut everyone up."

Dick Modzelewski

*on events leading up to the
1964 NFL title game*

These guys would throw a block at the line of scrimmage, then they'd get up, run 10 or 20 yards down the field, and nail someone else. It was common for Hickerson and Schafrath to throw three blocks on one play.

Jim Brown

The more we prepared for the Colts, the more we became convinced they couldn't beat us. It was the feeling of confidence.

Blanton Collier

*before the 1964 NFL
Championship Game
vs. Baltimore*

Cleveland totally dominated the Johnny Unitas-led Colts, in a major NFL championship upset, 27–0.

We don't want any butchers on this team. Don't eat with your elbows on the table, and don't make noise when you eat. Don't wear T-shirts to the dining room. If you are a drinker or a chaser, you weaken the team, and we don't want you. We're here for just one thing—to win.

Paul Brown

He preached to all the players, "When a kid asks you for an autograph, you better give it to him. If not, I'll make you do it." He believed that you meet the same people on the way up that you do on the way down, and you want to make sure you have a good relationship with them.

Jim Ray Smith
guard (1956–62),
on Lou Groza

Hell, yeah, you've got to be tough, and you're gonna get some licks. But I never even called time all the years I played. I'd wait until the end of the quarter or let someone else call time. I always had a full tank of gas.

Frank "Gunner" Gatski
Hall of Fame center (1946–56)

Paul Brown taught me about being a man. If I had not had my previous years with Cleveland, I wouldn't have made it in Washington.

Bobby Mitchell

Mitchell was traded after the 1961 season, along with the Browns' top pick in the upcoming college draft, to the Washington Redskins for the rights to the No. 1 overall selection—Syracuse Heisman Trophy winner Ernie Davis. In the nation's capital, Mitchell broke the Redskins' color barrier as their first-ever black signee. There, having switched to flankerback and finally out from under Jim Brown's huge shadow, Mitchell created his own Hall of Fame spotlight.

He would take over in the huddle. We were in a tight game once, and Gary Collins asked for a pass. Frank Ryan was hesitant about calling it, and Jim said, "Hey man, give the man the ball. He knows what he has, give him the ball." He was that kind of guy.

John Wooten

on Jim Brown

Sometimes, rather than ride the bus five miles to school, Schafrath said he would race it. He read that Jim Thorpe used to do the same thing. Dick Schafrath's search for new challenges never ceased. He used to wrestle Victor the Bear, who stood 11 feet tall and weighed 650 pounds.

John Keim

A babyhood bone deficiency left him, at age 8, with a left leg two inches shorter than the right. He had to wear a steel brace from hip to ankle, and each week for the next four years, the orthopedist would adjust a screw that stretched the leg. Mac Speedie's determination to become an athlete grew stronger. An inner toughness and resolve placed him on a different plateau from those around him.

Jack Clary

He had a competitive spirit to be able to lead a team. He just carried us on his back and said, "Let's go."

Ozzie Newsome
on Bernie Kosar

We really made practice like a game-type situation. Those guys [Browns receivers] used to take it easy, and other defensive backs let them catch the ball. Not Frank [Minnifield] and I. We really worked them. Our philosophy was, once they go against us, they were prepared to go against anyone.

Hanford Dixon

My grandfather used to tell me, "You can always find good in tragedy; you just have to look for it." The tragedy to me was God shorted me two inches. I despised that, but it was the motivation that I needed to help me play. I had to learn how to use size as an advantage.

Greg Pruitt

Pruitt, the 1972 Heisman Trophy runner-up from Oklahoma, stood 5–10 and weighed 190.

There are a lot of great players in the NFL, but I learned very quickly: Along with the talents they have, those players who play from the cerebral level are the ones who succeed at the highest level.

Paul Warfield

When you're riding the crest, a lot of things happen because someone makes great plays that are more or less accepted. When you make them with the chips down, that's when they are remembered.

Lou Groza

*Hall of Fame left tackle/
placekicker (1946–59, 1961–67)*

For me, as a Northeast Ohio kid, to play his last game on the Cleveland Browns field in front of Cleveland Browns fans in a Cleveland Browns helmet, I couldn't write it any better.

Chris Spielman

linebacker, who, after eight years with the Detroit Lions and two with Buffalo, closed out his distinguished NFL career with Cleveland. In the final game of the 1999 preseason, Spielman lay motionless after a helmet-to-helmet hit. He retired shortly thereafter

BROWNS
HUMOR

T HE BROWNS HAVE A quarterback who understands Einstein's theory of relativity and 10 other guys who didn't know there was one.

Jim Murray

late Los Angeles Times *columnist, referring to Frank Ryan's cerebral side, the part that earned a Ph.D. in mathematics from Rice University five months after winning the 1964 NFL championship*

Ryan's thesis at Rice was titled "Characterization of the Set of Asymptomatic Values of a Function Holomorphic in the Unit Disc."

Old Paul Brown, he threw nickels around as if they were manhole covers.

Gene Hickerson
guard (1958–60, 1962–73)

Paul Brown could be so cold that you'd get pneumonia just being in the same room with him.

Pete Franklin
Cleveland radio sports legend

No ties. It's a playoff, sudden death.

Blanton Collier
when asked by a player if the team was required to wear coats and ties while traveling to a warm-weather site for a playoff game. Collier was hard of hearing

He must mean that he's losing his hair.

Anonymous
on quarterback Frank Ryan's comment before the Pro Bowl Game in 1965 that he felt he could be another Y. A. Tittle

You rush Graham, put on a move and beat your man, and there's Motley waiting for you. Next play, you beat your man with a different move, and there's Motley waiting again. Pretty soon you say, "The hell with it. I'd rather stay on the line and battle the first guy."

Gail Bruce
San Francisco 49ers defensive end (1948–52)

Fair Hooker? I've never met one.

Don Meredith
former Dallas Cowboys quarterback/pioneering Monday Night Football *color analyst, on the Browns' receiver (1969–74) by that name, during the inaugural* MNF *telecast—Browns vs. Jets— Sept. 21, 1970*

I probably never will get in. There are a lot of players in the Hall of Fame that I know damn well I have a better track record than. I don't kiss asses with the voters and I never will. I'm in Burger King's Hall of Fame, and that's enough.

Gene Hickerson

Last season, I called almost a dozen plays for Cleveland.

Milt Plum

*quarterback (1957–61),
neglecting to mention the almost
850 plays run by the Browns that
were called by head coach Paul
Brown*

Tell the coaches and players to forget about practice and meetings today. It's too wet to do anything.

George Ratterman

quarterback (1952–56), to a Houston, Texas, hotel operator, where the Browns were housed. Ratterman at the time was part of an AAFC all-star team that played Cleveland after the 1949 season in Houston. A notorious practical joker, Ratterman later joined the Browns, mostly backing up Otto Graham during his five-year career in Cleveland

Ratterman once posted a notice on the team bulletin board notifying everyone that there would be a meeting of the "fake field goal holders." Naturally, a couple of players showed up, and several others asked Paul Brown where and what time.

Jack Clary

on another classic George Ratterman practical joke

My first home game in Cleveland, my rookie year, we got on our knees and said the Lord's Prayer, and as soon as we got through, someone—I think it was Bob Gain—jumped up and said, "Let's kill the sons of bitches!"

Jim Ray Smith

It's about time we played against a team whose owner is hated worse than ours.

Unidentified Houston Oilers Linebacker

Oilers (later Titans) boss Bud Adams, who relocated his team to Tennessee, incurred the same animosity and contempt from Houstonians as Art Modell experienced at the hands of Clevelanders in 1995.

You do that, and you'll have more brains in your belly than you have in your head.

Greg Pruitt

to Kansas City Chiefs defensive end Buck Buchanan, who had threatened that he would "bite [Pruitt's] head off," when Pruitt had wriggled for extra yardage after an initial stop by the future Hall of Famer

If he did have a big butt, he could carry 230–235 pounds and not lose speed. Rich came back and said, "Sam, he's got a big butt." From the day he came in, it was his job.

Sam Rutigliano

on 1978 future first-round draftee and eventual Hall of Fame tight end Ozzie Newsome. Rutigliano had sent assistant coach Rich Kotite to Tuscaloosa, Ala., asking him in particular to check out the size of the Alabama receiver's behind for the above-named reasons

I bet Dino's folks feel five feet tall.

Dave Graf

linebacker (1975–79),
on Dino Hall, the 5–7, 165-pound
Browns return man (1979–83),
who had an especially good day
on the field, with his parents in
the stands

Do you know how to become a millionaire from owning a sports team? Start out as a billionaire.

Art Modell

owner (1961–95)

I feel like a fireplug at a dog show.

Bob Golic

defensive tackle (1982–88),
on playing in front of the
notorious cluster of rabid
Browns fans in the Dawg Pound

BROWNS LEGENDS

THE PEOPLE WHO TALK about Marion Motley are talking about the Motley who played in the NFL—on two bad knees. The Motley they saw was just a shadow of the old Motley, even when he made All-Pro in 1950 and led the league in running. Don't forget, he was 26 years old in his rookie year in 1946.

Lou Saban

linebacker and defensive captain (1946–49)/former Denver Broncos head coach (1967–71)

Motley, the All-America Football Conference's all-time leading rusher, topped the NFL in rushing in 1950.

Nothing about Dante Lavelli was subtle, from his cocky, center-stage personality to the way he soared above defenders to snag Otto Graham passes. As one-half of the first great receiving tandem in pro football history, Lavelli helped lift the Cleveland Browns from All-America Football Conference infancy to NFL dominance.

Ron Smith

I think Lavelli has the strongest hands I've ever seen. When he goes up for a pass and a defender goes up with him, you can be sure Dante will have the ball when they come down. Nobody can ever take it away from him once he gets his hands on it.

Paul Brown

PHOTO COURTESY OF THE CLEVELAND BROWNS

Dante Lavelli

One year, I had 40 passes thrown to me and I caught every one of them.

Dante Lavelli
referring to his AAFC league-leading 40 receptions in 1946

He really did have glue fingers.

Otto Graham
on Dante Lavelli, whose nickname was "Glue Fingers"

Marion Motley was a human freight train when he carried the ball on sweeps or up the middle on his patented draws and trap plays. He was a relentless blocker on runs, a one-man wall for quarterback Otto Graham on passes and a capable receiver. He also was an outstanding linebacker.

Ron Smith

I tackled Motley head-on [on the first day of the Browns' 1946 training camp]. I felt like I was being hit by a truck. He had huge thighs. From that point on, I tried to tackle him from the side, drag him down. He was a load.

Lou Groza

There is no comparison between Jim Brown and Marion Motley. Motley was the greatest all-around fullback.

Otto Graham

Combine the mental toughness of Jackie Robinson with the skills of Ottis Anderson and Tom Rathman, and roll that into a 6–1, 238-pound ball. The result would be Marion Motley.

Peter King

Sports Illustrated

Motley really built the passing attack for the Browns because of his blocking.

Dante Lavelli

Marion Motley

PHOTO COURTESY OF THE CLEVELAND BROWNS

The greatest back I ever had was Marion Motley. The only statistic he ever knew was whether we won or lost. The man was completely unselfish.

Paul Brown

Brown included Jim Brown in his assessment, saying that the Hall of Fame fullback of the late-1950s to mid-'60s would have been Motley's equal had he worked on his blocking.

Jim Brown was the best pure runner I've ever seen, but Marion Motley was the greatest all-around player, the complete player. He ran. He caught flare passes and turned them into big gainers. He backed up the line in an era in which the rest of the world was switching to two platoons, and he pass-blocked like no other back who ever played the game.

Paul Zimmerman
author

If there is a better football player who ever snapped on a helmet, I would like to know his name.

Paul Zimmerman

on Marion Motley

Frank Gatski played every game, and took part in every practice, in high school, college, and the pros, a trend that continued when he played for Detroit for a season.

John Keim

According to Groza, Frank Gatski was the only center he ever saw pull on a trap play.

Ron Smith

He was an iron man. He came to work and just did his job. That was it.

Mike McCormack

Hall of Fame tackle/middle guard (1954–62),
on Frank Gatski

For several years, Gatski was the only center Cleveland took to training camp, an unheard of move then and now.

John Keim

He's in the Hall of Fame as much for his play as a lineman as for his placekicking.

Paul Brown

on Lou "The Toe" Groza

After drilling field goals of 49, 51, and 50 yards, the latter in a driving rainstorm in Miami, writers started calling him "Groza the Toe-za," which soon became the more famous "Lou the Toe."

John Keim

on Groza's legendary nickname, accrued during the Browns' first season, in 1946

As youngsters, my brother Frank and I used to practice placekicking by kicking a football over some telephone wires.

Lou Groza

Photo Courtesy of the Cleveland Browns

Lou Groza

I remember when the goal posts were on the goal line. One day Groza lined up to kick a 53-yard field goal. I said, "What's happening here? Do they have a trick play?" He made the kick, absolutely made it. I was seeing a new game.

Ara Parseghian
Browns halfback (1948–49)/
head coach at Notre Dame
(1964–74)

Lou Groza shortened the football field for us—from 100 yards to 60 yards.

Paul Brown

He's washed up. He's over the hill.

Paul Brown
on Lou Groza, prior to The Toe's
coming out of retirement in 1961

Groza kicked for another seven seasons, through 1967. In all, The Toe's tenure spanned 21 years as a Cleveland Brown, the longest in franchise history.

Bill Willis, a member of Paul Brown's 1942 Ohio State championship team, asked for a tryout with Brown's new All-America Football Conference team. Brown agreed and watched Willis bolt over, around, and through center Mo Scarry on four straight plays in a stunning training camp drill. No Browns player protested when Willis was signed as pro football's first black since the early 1930s.

Ron Smith

About the first guy that ever convinced me that I couldn't handle anybody I ever met was Bill Willis. They called him The Cat. He would jump right over you.

Bulldog Turner
Chicago Bears Hall of Fame center/linebacker

PHOTO COURTESY OF THE CLEVELAND BROWNS

Bill Willis

On defense, he became the real pioneer of what is now the middle linebacker. Sometimes we'd put him up as the center of a five-man line, but quite often, to take advantage of his speed and agility, we'd drop him back and allow him to go to the play. He had no peers through much of his professional career.

Paul Brown

on Bill Willis

I'm awfully sorry. I hope you understand I'm just doing my job.

Len Ford

Hall of Fame defensive end (1950–57), as he helped up Washington Redskins quarterback Eddie LeBaron, whom Ford had battered to the ground all afternoon during a game in the early 1950s

Wind him up and watch him destroy an offense. Len Ford was a defensive monster with incredible athleticism. At 6–5 and 260 pounds, he had linebacker speed, running back quickness, and an ability to leap high and bat down passes. When Cleveland coach Paul Brown got his hands on this 1950s prototype, he secured an important piece of his championship puzzle and unleashed a new kind of devastation on the NFL.

Ron Smith

I would say he and Gino Marchetti invented the pass rush.

Walt Michaels
*linebacker (1952–61),
on pioneering defensive end
Len Ford*

One of his favorite tricks was to throw a blocker at the quarterback.

Johnny Unitas

*Baltimore Colts Hall of Fame
quarterback,
on defensive end Doug Atkins
(1953–54)*

I considered myself the best guard of this century, and I played against some mean ones. But I never met anyone meaner than Atkins. After my first meeting with him, I really wanted to quit pro football.

Jim Parker

*Baltimore Colts Hall of Fame guard,
on Doug Atkins*

He never made a mistake; he always knew where he was supposed to be. He had tremendous leadership. If Captain Mike said something, that was it. It was like God speaking. We all looked up to him.

Bobby Mitchell

*Hall of Fame halfback
(1958–61),
on fellow Hall of Famer, tackle
Mike McCormack*

Nobody ruled the Cleveland trenches more skillfully than big-hearted Mike McCormack, a 6–4, 250-pound Irishman who was equal parts diplomat and enforcer.

Ron Smith

He had to step in for Bill Willis, but he also added a lot to the position. Bill had great quickness, but Mike had the size and speed. No one took any liberties with the middle of our defense, and when we turned him loose on the pass rush, he just crushed the middle of that passing pocket.

Howard Brinker
*assistant coach (1952–73),
on McCormack's first year with
the Browns at middle guard on
defense, before being converted
to right tackle on offense*

Jim Brown was a physical masterpiece, a gift from the football gods. His 18-inch neck, wide shoulders, and 45-inch chest tapered down to a 32-inch waist and massive thighs that carried him around the field with animal grace. Brown ran with head high, nostrils flaring, legs pumping and powerful arms swatting away tacklers like flies. He was an amazing combination of power and speed, a big cat who could juke past slower defenders or run over linebackers and defensive backs.

Ron Smith

He told me, "Make sure when anyone tackles you he remembers how much it hurts." He lived by that philosophy and I always followed that advice.

John Mackey
*Baltimore Colts Hall of Fame
tight end,
on Jim Brown*

He was the best basketball player, the best golfer, and, I'm sure, the best lacrosse player. Whatever it was, he would have been the best of anything he wanted to be. The aura around him was the same as around Muhammad Ali. If there was a guy who could have whipped Ali, it would have been Jim Brown.

Dale Lindsey
linebacker (1965–72)

Everything he did had a purpose. He was a thinking man's runner.

Paul Warfield
on Jim Brown

Jim was very easy to work with. He didn't ask for much, just get out of the way. He didn't need much help.

Gene Hickerson

I've never seen a back more endowed with all the things needed to rush the football. He was an amazing physical specimen who had the physique and an upper torso of a 250–260 pounder. And he was a finesse player. He never abused his power or strength. He was so nimble on his feet and athletic. He could catch the ball out of the backfield with one hand, he would throw the ball, and, on top of that, he was an extremely intelligent player. I was in tremendous awe. You'd see the film and see the things this guy did, and it was incredible. It was almost like no other human being could do them.

Paul Warfield

on Jim Brown

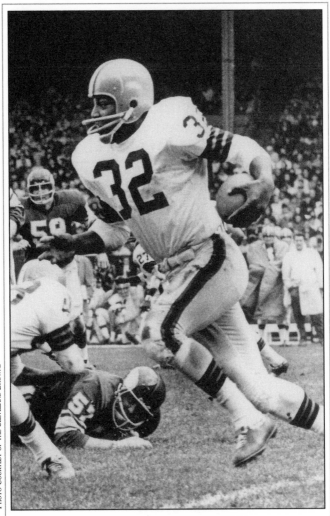

PHOTO COURTESY OF THE CLEVELAND BROWNS

Jim Brown

His feet were never far off the ground when he ran, so he was very difficult to knock down. Another key was the unusual muscle structure in his upper thighs that generated his power. . . . In a game, his great second efforts were his trademarks, and he never once complained to me, even after running 25 or 30 times a game.

Paul Brown
on Jim Brown

God made one running back. It was Jim Brown, and he threw the mold away.

Dick Modzelewski

If certain guys wanted to think I was otherworldly, I'd be the last man on earth to dissuade them. Mystique is a powerful force.

Jim Brown

After the 1965 season, the 30-year-old Brown shocked the football world by announcing his retirement, stating the football part of his life was over. Jim Brown left pro football as the NFL's all-time leading rusher. It would take 20 years before Chicago's Walter Payton would break Brown's yardage record.

Bob Italia
author

He had tremendous speed, the ability to shift his weight without faltering and he could stop and start at full speed. He became the greatest will-o'-the-wisp runner ever to play for my teams.

Paul Brown
on halfback Bobby Mitchell

He really terrified defenders.

Paul Warfield
on Bobby Mitchell

If not for Jim Brown, Mitchell would have been the centerpiece of a Cleveland offense that had dominated the NFL through much of the 1950s. But Brown handled the primary running load while Mitchell was used in change-of-pace situations and as a receiver out of the backfield.

Ron Smith
on Bobby Mitchell

Bobby maneuvered smoothly and possessed lightning speed. That was the greatest backfield of all time—Brown and Mitchell. When Mitchell made a cut, he didn't slow down.

Lou Groza

Paul Warfield very well may be the finest football prospect to hit training camp since Jim Brown crashed the scene in 1957.

Chuck Heaton
Plain Dealer, *1964*

Photo Courtesy of the Cleveland Browns

Bobby Mitchell

PHOTO COURTESY OF THE CLEVELAND BROWNS

Paul Warfield

Paul Warfield was one of the classiest people ever to wear a Browns uniform. You talk to him for five minutes, and you realize that he is as graceful in person as he was as a Hall of Fame wide receiver.

Terry Pluto

Paul was so fluid, he was like an antelope.

Dick Schafrath
on Warfield

Paul gave us a dimension we didn't have before. He was so fast and great at getting open. He was a guy who could catch a pass and go 80 yards for a touchdown.

Frank Ryan
*quarterback (1962–68),
on Warfield*

The misfortune of Paul Warfield is that he never got a chance to play in a passing offense.

Ron Smith

Gary Collins was equal to Warfield as a receiver, but if Gary was open, he needed to be way open to score. He had good speed, but not blinding speed like Paul. Now we had receivers on both sides of the line who were tremendous threats, and we had Jim Brown in the backfield. It just opened up the field for us.

Frank Ryan

When Leroy Kelly became a starter in 1966, it made me that much more effective as a receiver. He was an excellent pass catcher, so the defense couldn't concentrate on me. He froze a lot of linebackers.

Paul Warfield

Maybe I was dumb or ignorant, but I just didn't feel the pressure of replacing Jim Brown. We had great coaches, a great offensive line, and a great team. I had enough confidence to know I could do it, barring injury.

Leroy Kelly
running back (1964–1973)

The signs were there that he could play. No one really knew, however. He not only played well, he instantly became, along with Gale Sayers, one of the top two running backs in the league.

Paul Warfield
on Leroy Kelly

Leroy Kelly was like a cat. So was Jim Brown, only a bigger cat. It's difficult to knock a cat off his feet.

Ernie Green
running back (1962–68)

He was a Cadillac with a blue-collar mentality.

Calvin Hill
running back (1978–81),
on Hall of Fame guard
Joe DeLamielleure

He's a human highlight reel on how to play guard in the NFL.

Mike Giddings
personnel evaluator,
on Joe DeLamielleure (1980–84)

Ozzie Newsome was a wide receiver trapped in a tight end's body. Cleveland coach Sam Rutigliano drafted the 6–2, 230-pound Alabama wideout in 1978 and introduced him to a new position. In his first pro game, the first time he touched the ball, Newsome sprinted 33 yards for a touchdown on a reverse.

Ron Smith

6

PAUL BROWN U.

No one, I mean no one, has ever had total command and respect like Paul Brown. Not Lombardi, not Landry, none of them. I believe that Paul Brown could have been a general in the army . . . he could have taken over Ford Motor Company or IBM.

Paul Wiggin

Paul Brown was pro football.

Terry Pluto

Paul Brown

PHOTO COURTESY OF THE CLEVELAND BROWNS

He was the first coach for two inaugural NFL franchises and an innovator who affected the course of pro football's evolution. Paul Brown is best remembered as a ground-breaking pro football pioneer. He introduced player intelligence testing and film evaluation. He made scouting a fulltime, year-round profession. He was the first to keep extra players on "taxi squads," the first to shuttle plays to quarterbacks and the first to run scrimmage-free practices. The two-minute drill was a Brown brainstorm, as were the draw play, sideline and screen passes, and the facemask.

Ron Smith

He also was the first to consistently use a number of black players. Paul Brown also won.

Terry Pluto

Today a player's time in the 40-yard dash is a universally accepted measure of a football player's speed. But it was Paul Brown who used it first. Believing that the average punt went 40 yards, he wanted to see how fast his defensive players could go that distance to cover the punt.

Terry Pluto

As each year goes by, I gain more respect for Paul Brown. The world could use more Paul Browns.

Otto Graham

Paul Brown was the coach of all coaches.

Jim Ray Smith

In 1940, his Massillon [Ohio] High School Tigers scrimmaged Kent State University. They scored more than 50 points before Kent State stopped the carnage in the fourth quarter.

John Keim

Then he did it at Ohio State, winning the 1942 national championship. At the Great Lakes Naval Academy, he took a team patched together before the season that was good enough by year's end to beat Notre Dame, 39–7. Brown later placed that win alongside his greatest of all time.

John Keim

Everything was built on a Spartan, tough, fight-your-way-to-the-death basis. As the attitude seeped into our players, they began to realize they didn't need any comforts on the field.

Paul Brown

There got to be a saying: "There's a right way, a wrong way, and the Paul Brown way." If you did it the Paul Brown way, you were right.

Kenny Konz
safety (1953–59)

Paul was tough. Everybody should have to play one year under Paul.

John Wooten

I loved the guy 90 percent of the time and hated his guts 10 percent of the time.

Otto Graham

on Paul Brown

With Lombardi, he would cuss you and jump all over you and after he got through with you, you felt beat up. But Paul would get on you and say it in such a way that you'd just walk away and all of a sudden realize you're bleeding to death.

Mike McCormack

I'm glad I came into the league with Paul Brown. I needed the father figure, the disciplinarian and a man who believed in family, who said how you should treat your wife and kids. He was an innovator, and he made great ball-players out of a lot of guys who wouldn't have been that good.

Bobby Mitchell

There are many times when I think I am a liability to my team. It seems that every time we meet a team where one of my former players or coaches is my counterpart, they try harder to beat me than they do my team. I hate to think of myself as someone else's incentive.

Paul Brown

Coaching under Paul Brown is like living next to a library. I'd be a fool not to check any books out.

Sam Wyche

head coach, Cincinnati Bengals
(1984–91)

Tomorrow it may be hot and we'll practice. Later there will be snow and we'll practice. It may be raining buckets and we'll practice. Soon you'll accept this as a part of the routine and enjoy it.

Paul Brown

to his players each year
at training camp

Keep your wives out of football. Don't have your wife talk football with other wives. It breeds trouble.

Paul Brown

Paul Brown had a "no sex after Tuesday" rule. Wives making road trips stayed in a separate hotel from the players.

Duey Graham
author

If you're cut from the squad, be a man about it. We can't keep everybody.

Paul Brown

Paul didn't adjust to the changes in the game. By 1962, he was more worried about protecting his reputation as the Greatest Coach Who Ever Lived than he was about winning a title.

Bernie Parrish
cornerback (1959–66)

I don't think Art Modell wanted to fire Paul Brown because he was sensitive to public opinion, but the more he heard from the players, he knew he had to fire Paul Brown.

Bill Glass
defensive end (1962–68)

It broke his heart when he was fired. There has always been a lot of talk and rationalizations [about the firing], but it came down to the fact that Art Modell wanted to run the Browns and couldn't as long as my father was there.

Mike Brown

Paul Brown's son and longtime president/general manager, Cincinnati Bengals

It was like the Terminal Tower toppling.

Frank Gibbons

Cleveland Press,
on the firing of Paul Brown at the end of the 1962 season

The Tower was Cleveland's tallest building until 1991 and remains a major city landmark.

The dismissal of Paul Brown is a move that defies comprehension. The moody genius from the lakefront had achieved an eminence in his profession that lifted him far above the pack, virtually exalting him to a class by himself. If he was unloved, he was admired and respected by all. He was a man who built a better mousetrap.

Arthur Daley
The New York Times

I really believe that part of the reason the players performed so well for Blanton [Collier] is that they wanted to justify Paul's firing.

Bob August
Cleveland Press,
*who covered the Browns
from 1953 through 1957*

Most of the decisions Paul made were the right decisions. That's what gave him the strength and the discipline that he had. That's what made him a fine coach.

Dub Jones
halfback/receiver (1948–55)

My satisfaction was proving my principals, proving that the same ideals that won in high school and college could win in professional ball.

Paul Brown

SHRINE TO NO. 14

HE WAS A WINNING machine.

Ron Smith

*on Hall of Fame quarterback
Otto Graham*

To me, winning never has been the most important thing. The desire to win—putting forth the effort to win—that is the most important thing.

Otto Graham

Automatic Otto was just that from 1946 through 1949 when he led the Browns to a 47–4–3 record and four straight championships in the All-America Football Conference, and from 1950 through 1955 when his Browns captured three NFL titles and lost three other times in the title game. Ten straight championship-game appearances and a 105–17–4 ten-year record are legacies unmatched by any other quarterback.

Ron Smith

He was one of the great football players of all time. He could have played today for any team out there.

Tony Adamle
on Graham

He was the perfect quarterback for the near-perfect franchise.

Ron Smith

PHOTO COURTESY OF THE CLEVELAND BROWNS

Otto Graham

The amazing part of the Otto Graham story is the fact that he wasn't even invited out for the football team his freshman year [at Northwestern]. Through the grapevine, word reached the football coaching staff that there was a freshman playing in the intramural league who could really toss the football.

Bill Levy
author

Otto Graham was an All-American in football and basketball, an eight-letter man at Northwestern. In 1943, he led the College All-Stars to victory over the Washington Redskins. He was also talented in music.

James V. Young
Arthur F. McClure
authors

I had a musical background [his father, Otto Sr., taught music]. I wish I'd been smart; I could still be playing the piano if I'd kept up with it, or the violin, cornet, or the French horn [Otto, an all-state French horn player in high school at Waukegan, Ill., was then 74]. I tell kids, "Don't be a damn fool like me. Keep up your music. Years later, you'll be the hit of the party, whereas guys like me can't do anything but sit around." I was watching the Three Tenors sing. I get chills listening to those guys. If I could sing like that, my godamighty, you could take all these damn trophies and melt 'em down, for all I'd care. When I played music, I played because I *had* to. I played with a brass sextet that won first place in a national contest in Columbus, Ohio. But I have to tell you, they didn't win because of me. Those guys were the real stars. I just went "oom-pah-pah."

Otto Graham

I don't go for this hot-dogging stuff. I don't mind guys pumping their fists in the end zone, but this planned stuff, where you're wiggling your knees, or turning flips, or waiting for four or five guys to show up and do all these gyrations...I'll guarantee you if I was coaching today, every time anyone did that, they'd be fined at least $10,000. Every damn time. As Paul Brown used to say, "Act like you've been there before." I don't see why the league doesn't step in and really crack down on this kind of stuff.

Otto Graham

His legs were so long Graham could stand erect to take snaps, allowing him better vision of defensive alignments.

Ron Smith

I remember his tremendous peripheral vision and his great athletic skill, as well as his ability to throw a football far and accurately with just a flick of his arm.

Paul Brown

The one thing I could do as a quarterback was throw the ball as accurately as anybody in the history of the game. But I couldn't throw the ball as long or maybe as hard, or I couldn't run as fast as a lot of quarterbacks.

Otto Graham

I didn't know Bobby that well when we played against each other. I got to know him very well afterwards; I liked him very much. He was a happy-go-lucky guy. I don't condone the way he lived his life; he didn't train that well, but he was a great competitor—his teammates loved him. He would chew them out on the field like mad, but they knew damn well it was for their own good, because he wanted to win. After the game, it was all forgotten. All his guys knew that if they screwed up, he wouldn't buy 'em a beer after the game. We were different people, but, boy, he was a great competitor.

Otto Graham

on Detroit Lions Hall of Fame quarterback Bobby Layne

I made a dive for Graham and hit him with my elbow. I hope he's all right. I sure didn't mean to hit him.

Art Michalik

San Francisco 49ers middle guard, on his out-of-bounds hit to the face that opened a three-inch gash, resulting in 15 stitches for Graham during the Browns–49ers game of 1953. Graham was taken to the locker room and sewn up, without Novocain, returning to hit on nine of 10 passes in the second half, in leading Cleveland to a 23–21 victory. Retaliation by the Browns was swift: Both of Michalik's eyes were blackened by game's end

Your breath would bounce back into your face. It was hard to breathe, and your vision was impaired because it wasn't transparent. You could see everything above and below, but there was a hell of a lot of field you couldn't see.

Otto Graham

on the impromptu face mask created for him by equipment manager Morrie Kono, at Paul Brown's insistence, after Graham survived an elbow to the face requiring 15 stitches in a 1953 game against San Francisco. Graham's curved plastic bar, though not the first face protection worn in the NFL, led directly to the advent of the modern face mask

Paul Brown solicited help from Riddell, the sports equipment manufacturer, to devise a protective bar for the helmet in the off-season following Graham's injury. The company's initial prototype cracked in cold weather and also fogged up, but shortly thereafter, Riddell came up with an acceptable one-inch-diameter face bar that everyone began wearing.

How you build yourself emotionally is a big factor. With football being a contact sport, you gotta go out and hit people. You gotta have confidence. If you get off to a good start and you keep going, you get a lot of confidence, and if you're confident, it gives you a lot more yards, I guarantee you. The mind is so important.

Otto Graham

Otto was the main reason the Browns were called the team of the 1950s. He had an awful lot of talent; he was a great guy in the huddle and a great team man.

Mike McCormack

Today they basically babysit the quarterbacks, because they can't afford to get 'em hurt. That being said, I'm a firm believer that the athlete of today is better than the athlete of my day, in all sports. They're bigger, faster, stronger. Sure, the good guys of my day could play today, but we didn't have weight-training programs and that kind of stuff. We'd have done alright, but a good, big player will beat a good, small player.

Otto Graham

His teammates liked him because Graham never tried to place himself above them.

John Keim

I didn't like it. The white ball had two black stripes on it, on either end. The stripe was right where I'd place my thumb. It was very slippery, very hard to grip the ball. It made it tough to throw. And the balls back then were a little larger, too. No, I didn't like it. You were affected mentally by it.

Otto Graham

*on the white football used
for night games in the 1940s
and '50s*

He's the greatest thing to come out of Waukegan since Jack Benny.

**Anonymous description
of Otto Graham**

*on the quarterback's and
comedian's hometown
Illinois roots*

The highlight of my whole career was that first year in the NFL, in 1950, the season opener. For four years, Paul Brown never said a word about the NFL to us. He would just take all those derogatory comments made by commissioners and coaches and players and sportswriters and put them on the bulletin board, so that we could read them and let it soak in. By the time that game rolled around with the big, two-time defending world's champion Philadelphia Eagles, Paul Brown didn't have to do one thing to get us up emotionally. Hell, he had to keep us toned down, if anything. We just went out there and demolished them. We even had two touchdowns called back. We killed 'em.

Otto Graham

The Browns defeated Philadelphia, in one of the most famous games in NFL history, 35–10. Graham's sterling performance included 346 passing yards and three scoring aerials.

Graham's ghost hovered ever near in the collective subconsciouness, a doppelganger in white leather helmet, facemaskless, wearing basketball shoes for traction on frozen turf, darting past befuddled defenders, unleashing prodigious throws that bolted from his hand like startled gamebirds and arched into smoky winter skies as chilly as gray aspic, then folded their necks and hunched their shoulders and fell feathery onto fingertips. Always.

Alan Natali

author,
on the Browns' extensive search
to fill Otto Graham's huge shoes

The thing is, Otto could've played for a couple more years and still been on top. But he evidently got tired of traveling and the pressure to keep winning. All the players wanted him to come back, and he finally decided he didn't want to do it. I think we'd have won again if he'd have come back!

Dante Lavelli

John Elway makes in one game what I made in my whole career.

Otto Graham

The thing that I should be known for more than anything else is that Vince Lombardi replaced me as head coach of the Washington Redskins.

Otto Graham

MAJOR MOMENTS

I ASSURE YOU, THERE'S never been a team in the history of sports that was better prepared emotionally to play a game than we were. We could have played them for a keg of beer or, in my case, a chocolate milk shake, just to prove we were a good team.

Otto Graham

on the buildup to the 1950 season opener against the two-time defending NFL champion Philadelphia Eagles, the Browns' first-ever game in the senior circuit after four years of dominance in the All-America Football Conference

When the final week of preparation came, we were ready. In fact, I lived in fear all week that we'd blow too soon. That game had been living inside us for so long it hardly seemed possible we could hold off another day. And when the game was played, we were the best football team I ever have seen. We had waited and thought about playing that game for three years and were at a razor's edge. Every action we made that night was perfect.

Paul Brown

on the 1950 season opener, Sept. 16, against Philadelphia. In a shocker, Cleveland trounced the Eagles, 35–10, in one of the classic contests in pro football history

It was like trying to cover three Don Hutsons . . . impossible . . . impossible.

Russ Craft

Philadelphia Eagles defensive back, on the trio of Browns receivers— Mac Speedie, Dante Lavelli, Dub Jones—that totally overwhelmed the Eagles, in Cleveland's first regular-season game in the NFL, the Browns' historic 35–10 defeat of Philadelphia

After that big win over the Eagles, there was all this business about "they're nothing but a basketball team," because the Eagles said we threw the ball so much. The next time we played 'em we didn't throw a single pass. The papers all said it was by design, but I wasn't aware of it, frankly. It was raining that day. It was a horrible day to throw the ball anyway. We just ran the ball down their throats and beat 'em again. The papers tried to put words in Paul's mouth, saying he was out to prove that we were more than a passing team. If our coaches planned it that way, we sure weren't aware of it. He was capable of doing it just for spite, but I have no knowledge of it being done on purpose.

Otto Graham

on the second game with the Eagles in 1950, Cleveland's 13–7 win in the rain and mud at Municipal Stadium

It was a silly grandstand play. It's amazing when you think we could go through a whole game without throwing a pass and still not lose our offensive momentum. Our players were good enough to do it any way we planned. I don't think Greasy Neale really ever forgave us for that.

Paul Brown

*on the Dec. 3, 1950, meeting
with Philadelphia, a 13–7 victory
produced without benefit of an
official pass*

I knew it meant the ball game. I just had to catch him. But I didn't think I had him in time. I thought we'd both probably be over the goal line. I just closed my eyes and grabbed for him.

Bill Willis

on his game-saving, come-from-behind tackle of New York Giants halfback Gene "Choo Choo" Roberts at the Cleveland 4 in the 1950 American Conference playoff game, after Roberts's fourth-quarter 32-yard dash. The magnificent defensive play by the team's fleet middle guard preserved what ultimately would be an 8–3 Cleveland victory. The win advanced the Browns to the NFL Championship Game against the Rams

On consecutive plays, Len Ford nailed Verda T. "Vitamin T" Smith for a 14-yard loss; sacked Bob Waterfield for 11 more yards; and tackled Glenn Davis for another 13 in arrears.

John Keim

on the phenomenal series of downs by the Browns' great Hall of Fame defensive end, upon entering the 1950 NFL title game against Los Angeles late in the first half. Ford had been sidelined for nine weeks due to a broken jaw sustained from the elbow of Chicago Cardinals fullback Pat Harder. He had lost 25 pounds since the Harder incident, and Paul Brown wasn't expecting much from Ford's play that Christmas Eve afternoon

If I could have found a hole, I would have crawled in and hid.

Otto Graham

after fumbling in the 1950 NFL Championship Game against the Los Angeles Rams with under three minutes to go and Cleveland behind, 28–27

Don't worry, Otts, we're still going to get them.

Paul Brown

to an agonized Otto Graham after the above-mentioned fumble. Brown was right. After shutting the Rams down on three plays and forcing a punt, Graham did get them, leading the renewed Browns on a climactic drive to the Rams 11, from where Lou Groza kicked a 16-yard field goal to cap the Brown's first NFL championship, 30–28

I'll never forget the time Dub Jones scored six touchdowns against the Chicago Bears in 1951. I overheard someone say, "Dub only needs one more touchdown to tie the all-time record." We finally got the ball and Paul sent me in with a certain play to run. This was one of the times I didn't choose to follow his recommendation. I told Dub to fake a Z-out shallow and go deep. He took the ball right on his finger tips and headed for the goal. Dub tied the record and Paul never said a word.

Otto Graham

They just beat the hell out of us.

Bobby Layne

on Detroit's 56–10 NFL Championship Game landslide loss to Cleveland in 1954. Layne was intercepted six times and the Lions fumbled away the ball three times

The game was a grudge match. It was a players' game. We wanted to show everyone—maybe ourselves most of all—that we were still good players. We had been written off and so had some of our coaches. We didn't like the image and simply responded to the challenge.

Dub Jones

on the Browns' 56–10 whitewash of the Detroit Lions in the 1954 NFL Championship Game

The defense, which had shown only a four-man rush the week before [in a 14–10 regular-season finale loss to Detroit], tore Bobby Layne's offense apart. Len Ford and Kenny Konz each intercepted two passes and the Browns had six in all, in addition to recovering three Detroit fumbles.

Jack Clary
on the Browns' 1954 NFL title conquest of Detroit

Twice—against Philadelphia and Pittsburgh—he grabbed the goalposts by his elbow and swung around to change directions on a slippery field and catch a touchdown pass. That trick resulted in the game-winning score with less than a minute remaining against the Eagles in a 21–17 win at home in 1955.

John Keim
on Dante Lavelli

Lenny was still going a little sideways, trying to turn the corner. I got a good angle on him, and I took him down.

Galen Fiss

on his tackle of Baltimore's Lenny Moore in the 1964 NFL title game. Fiss roll-blocked the future Hall of Fame halfback on a screen pass for a five-yard first-quarter loss that helped establish the defensive tone for the Browns, who shut out the Colts that afternoon 27–0

The largest crowd ever for a Browns game—85,703—saw Cleveland beat Joe Namath and the New York Jets, 31–21, on the first *Monday Night Football* game, September 21, 1970.

Tim Long
author

Terry was a big, strong guy, and he would keep struggling. The next thing I know, Joe picked him up and dumped him on his head. He looked like a chicken with his head cut off, and his [Bradshaw's] body flinched two or three times. It was something.

Thom Darden

on Joe "Turkey" Jones's legendary hit on Steelers QB Terry Bradshaw, Oct. 10, 1976, during an 18–16 Cleveland win

That was just awesome. If I could put time in a capsule, that would be the one night I would put in there.

Thom Darden

on the resounding 26–7 victory over Dallas on Monday Night Football, *Sept. 24, 1979, in which Darden made two interceptions, returning one for a touchdown. The win pushed Cleveland's Kardiac Kids to a heady 4–0 record*

At one point during the year, I remember yelling out, "Fasten your seatbelts! Here we go again!" That was the most fun I've ever had.

Gib Shanley

former Browns radio broadcaster,
during the 1980 season, in the Kardiac Kids era

Fans began talking Super Bowl, or, in some cases, Siper Bowl.

John Keim

Week after week, we dug ourselves a hole. But it was like, "OK, who's going to do whatever we need to do to win the game?" We didn't know how it was going to happen or when it was going to happen. But it was going to happen. And it happened. It was a magical year.

Greg Pruitt

on the Kardiac Kids, 1980

Sometimes I say to myself, "Was I really there? Was I really part of it?" It was just a great group of guys with a real resourceful quarterback. We were truly entertaining. As much as I had to pinch myself sometimes, I really savored and enjoyed it.

Sam Rutigliano

on the Kardiac Kids days

It was like an atomic bomb had been dropped over that whole place. That silence is something you never forget.

Ozzie Newsome

on the moment of death for the Kardiac Kids: Oakland safety Mike Davis's game-ending end-zone interception of Brian Sipe's pass intended for Newsome that gave the Oakland Raiders a 14–12 playoff win over the Browns, Jan. 4, 1981

I had beat Mike [Davis] so cleanly off the line of scrimmage that Sipe did what he was supposed to do. He was going to me. Mike made a great recovery, running for his life, and he looks up and there the ball is.

Ozzie Newsome

There would have been a monument to me in center field. Instead, it's just Red Right 88.

Sam Rutigliano

musing on the many "what ifs" of his infamous play call—Red Right 88—at the end of the 1980 playoff game against Oakland. On the play, quarterback Brian Sipe failed to spot a wide-open Dave Logan, instead forcing a pass to Ozzie Newsome. Raiders safety Mike Davis, initially beaten by Newsome, made a remarkable recovery to render the game-killing pick that preserved a 14–12 Raiders win and brought about the sudden and shocking end of the amazing Kardiac Kids era

It breaks my heart that I didn't come through. I made a bad throw. But that's exactly what we did that whole year and the year before. That's what made us the Kardiac Kids.

Brian Sipe
quarterback (1972–1983)

That ranks as one of the greatest games of all time. Just before we said our prayer in the locker room, I told the players to listen. You could still hear the people cheering for us. This is a victory, a game, a moment all of us will remember the rest of our lives.

Marty Schottenheimer
*head coach (1984–88),
on the Brown's thrilling 23–20
double-overtime victory over the
New York Jets, Jan. 3, 1987.
Cleveland, down by 10 points
with just 4:14 remaining, rallied
behind Bernie Kosar for the
improbable win*

The Drive was like a slow death, like you were being tortured.

Mike Trivisonno

WTAM–100 sports talk show host, on the legendary John Elway-led 98-yard drive to tie the 1986 AFC Championship Game between Cleveland and Denver at 20-all. The Broncos won in overtime on a 33-yard Rich Karlis field goal

I had always thought that if [Broncos wide receiver Steve] Watson had been another three or four inches short on the motion, that thing would have hit him right in the hip. It would have been a fumble, and who knows what would have happened in the game. That's the one play that stands out in my mind.

Marty Schottenheimer

referring to Elway's conversion of a third-and-18 pass to Mark Jackson during The Drive, with 1:47 remaining. On the play, Denver's Watson, sent in motion, passed by the center snap so close that the ball grazed his leg on its way back to Elway in shotgun formation. Schottenheimer's "what-if" musing was based on the conjecture that if Watson had started in motion another half-second later, in all probability the ball would have bounded off him, creating a fumble that might have wound up in Cleveland hands

I told the cameraman, "This is unbelievable. They're going to the Super Bowl." He said, "Hold on, not yet." Then they kick off and I watched Elway. I walked along the Broncos' sidelines, and he was just magic. That day he was the best I've ever seen. I really believe in my heart that if they [Cleveland] win that game, they beat the Giants in the Super Bowl. The Browns were as physical as any NFC team that year. It stays with me today. That one was tough to take. That's why a lot of people in Cleveland today still hate Elway. As much as I disliked him that day, I had to respect him for what he did.

Vince Cellini

CNN Headline News, formerly with the Cleveland CBS affiliate

The streak meant a lot to me, and it was something I really came to be identified with. We would get into the third quarter, and if I didn't have a catch, the fans would start chanting. And I knew Brian [Sipe] or Bernie [Kosar] would make sure I got that catch.

Ozzie Newsome

on his 150-consecutive-game streak with at least one catch, at the time the fourth-longest string in NFL history

The Buffalo Bills stood on the 11-yard line, running an offense the Browns couldn't stop. Nine seconds remained. This was Cleveland. This was the play-offs. This was the time to fall apart. Except it didn't happen. For once, the Browns received the breaks. Linebacker Clay Matthews knew the play, mainly because he had been beaten at least four times on it already. Thurman Thomas was the inside man in a three-receiver set. . . . Jim Kelly forced the ball over the middle at Matthews, who cradled it as he fell to his knee.

John Keim

on the game-sealing interception by Clay Matthews that preserved Cleveland's 34–30 divisional playoff victory over Buffalo in the 1989 postseason

It was the biggest play in a game of big plays.

Marv Levy

Buffalo Bills Hall of Fame head coach,
on Eric Metcalf's 90-yard kickoff return for a touchdown that boosted the Browns' lead over Buffalo to 31–21 in the third quarter of the 1989 AFC divisional playoff eventually won by Cleveland, 34–30

It was good by a coat of paint.

Matt Bahr

placekicker (1981–89), on his game-winning field goal in the Browns' payback 16–13 win against Denver during the 1989 regular season, their first victory over the Broncos since 1974 after a string of 10 successive defeats, including the AFC title game losses to Denver in 1986 and '87. Postseason failure again awaited Cleveland, though, as Denver, for the third time in four years, beat the Browns in the 1989 AFC Championship Game

I never wanted the day to be over.

Tony Jones

left tackle (1988–95),
after the Browns' final game in
Cleveland, Dec. 17, 1995, a
26–10 victory over Cincinnati.
Jones visited the Dawg Pound at
the game's conclusion, before
kneeling at midfield in a prayer
of thanks for having played
eight years in Cleveland

Long after the details—the score [43–0] and the grim reality that the first touchdown in the beautiful new Cleveland Browns Stadium was scored by Kordell Stewart of the rival Steelers—become fodder for trivia buffs, the evening of September 12, 1999, will be remembered as one of Cleveland's proudest moments.

Tim Graham

author,
on the Browns' opening-night return
to Cleveland, following three
seasons without a team, after the
original franchise under Art Modell
moved to Baltimore after 1995

9

CLEVELAND BROWNS ALL-TIME TEAM

*I*NEVITABLY, THE AGONY/JOY *of selecting an all-time team becomes an exercise in creativity. It would be blasphemous to leave a Marion Motley or a Bobby Mitchell off such an aggregation, so one looks deeper into their glittering resumes.*

Motley, considered by none other than Paul Brown as the best fullback in Cleveland Browns history, including Jim Brown, was also an impregnable force at linebacker, a position he brilliantly manned while a two-way star for Cleveland in the early AAFC days and on goal-line stands throughout his eight-year career.

Mitchell, frankly, was the best halfback I ever saw, before his conversion to flanker with Washington. Paul Brown's headstrong audacity in trading the dazzling, if occasionally fumbling, speedster still shakes heads among Browns supporters more than 40 years later, its place in the Ernie Davis tragedy from every angle an eternal riddle.

And wouldn't Dick Schafrath have made anybody else's all-time team at left tackle, except in Cleveland, where an untouchable Toe will forever man the spot?

One all-time position is immutable: mascot. The Brownie elf, its 34-year banishment at the cold heart of Art Modell notwithstanding, still rules.

Browns All-Time Team

Offense

DANTE LAVELLI, *wide receiver*
LOU GROZA, *tackle*
JIM RAY SMITH, *guard*
FRANK GATSKI, *center*
GENE HICKERSON, *guard*
MIKE MCCORMACK, *tackle*
OZZIE NEWSOME, *tight end*
PAUL WARFIELD, *wide receiver*
OTTO GRAHAM, *quarterback*
JIM BROWN, *running back*
LEROY KELLY, *running back*

Defense

LEN FORD, *defensive end*
MICHAEL DEAN PERRY, *defensive tackle*
JERRY SHERK, *defensive tackle*
BILL GLASS, *defensive end*
CLAY MATTHEWS, *linebacker*
BILL WILLIS, *middle guard/middle linebacker*
MARION MOTLEY, *linebacker*
WARREN LAHR, *cornerback*
THOM DARDEN, *free safety*
CLARENCE SCOTT, *strong safety*
FRANK MINNIFIELD, *cornerback*

Specialists

HORACE GILLOM, *punter*
LOU GROZA, *kicker*
ERIC METCALF, *punt returner*
BOBBY MITCHELL, *kick returner*

PAUL BROWN, *head coach*

DANTE LAVELLI
End (1946–56)
Pro Bowls (3), All-AAFC (2), All-NFL (2),
Hall of Fame (1975)

I can't remember him dropping a single pass, either in a game or practice. The reason was his great concentration on the ball and the best pair of hands I've ever seen on any receiver. They had an almost liquid softness which seemed to slurp the ball into them. He always seemed to catch every ball that was thrown near him.

Paul Brown
on Dante Lavelli

If I had to throw a ball to one individual in a clutch situation, I would pick Dante Lavelli.

Otto Graham

LOU GROZA
Tackle (1946–59, 1961–67)
Pro Bowls (9), All-NFL (6),
NFL Co-Player of the Year (1954),
Hall of Fame (1974)

Lou Groza was a placekicking pioneer who just happened to double as an All-Pro caliber offensive tackle. He could open up holes for the Cleveland Browns' machine-like offense and then cap a drive with a 40-yard field goal. He was a point-producing luxury in the era of 33-man rosters.

Ron Smith

Consider: He's the only Brown to play in all 13 of their championship games, including four in the AAFC and nine in the NFL. And he was the only one to play with, or for, 12 of Cleveland's 14 Hall of Famers.

John Keim
on Lou Groza

JIM RAY SMITH
Guard (1956–62)
Pro Bowls (5) consensus All-Pro (4)

Any of those old Browns will tell you the best player they had there was Jim Ray Smith. They'll say he was the best athlete they ever played with.

Dale Lindsey

He was the prototype offensive lineman. I'd come out with the ball, and he was the first one I'd look for. He was awesome. I've been fussing for years about this guy getting in the Hall.

Bobby Mitchell

FRANK GATSKI
Center (1946–56)
All-NFL (4), Hall of Fame (1985)

He was the best and the toughest I ever played against. As a linebacker, I sometimes had to go over the center, but Frank Gatski was an immovable object.

Chuck Bednarik
Hall of Fame center/linebacker, Philadelphia Eagles

GENE HICKERSON
Guard (1958–60, 1962–73)
Pro Bowls (6), All-Pro (5)

He's the reason I'm in the Hall of Fame. He should be in the Hall right now. I don't know why he's not. He put three running backs in there.

Leroy Kelly
Hall of Fame running back (1964–73), on Gene Hickerson

MIKE MCCORMACK
Tackle (1954–62)
Pro Bowls (5), All-NFL (2), Hall of Fame (1984)

Mike McCormack is the finest offensive tackle who ever played professional football. We could have played him at middle linebacker or on the defensive line, but his No. 1 niche was offensive right tackle. He was an excellent pass protector, but he could also blow people out of there.

Paul Brown

OZZIE NEWSOME
Tight End (1978–90)
Pro Bowls (3), All-Pro (2),
Hall of Fame (1999)

I knew if I threw the ball anywhere near Ozzie, he was probably going to catch it.

Bernie Kosar
on Ozzie Newsome

If there's a tight end that could catch the ball better than Ozzie Newsome, I haven't seen him. He had the best hands of any tight end I've ever seen.

Dave Logan
wide receiver (1976–83)

PAUL WARFIELD
Wide Receiver (1964–69, 1976–77)
Pro Bowls (3), All-Pro (3),
Hall of Fame (1983)

He was like the Michael Jordan of receivers. He'd just glide through his patterns. You'd swear his feet weren't even touching the ground. He was so smooth, he had to be flying.

Tom Melody

Akron Beacon Journal,
on Paul Warfield

Paul Warfield's pass routes weren't diagrammed; they were choreographed. His graceful, prancing style seemed more appropriate for a ballet than a football field.

Ron Smith

OTTO GRAHAM
Quarterback (1946–55)
Pro Bowls (5), All-AAFC (4), All-NFL (5),
AAFC Player of the Year (1947, '48),
NFL Player of the Year (1951, '53, '55),
NFL Championship Game MVP (1954, '55),
Pro Bowl MVP (1951), Hall of Fame (1965)

Otto was the greatest of all quarterbacks and my greatest player. For 10 years he propelled his team to 10 championship games. I don't discount Marion Motley, Dante Lavelli, or Jim Brown. But the guy that was the engineer, the guy with the touch that pulled us out of many situations was Otto Graham.

Paul Brown

Otto Graham was the Joe Montana of his era.

Terry Pluto

JIM BROWN
Running Back (1957–65)
Pro Bowls (9), All-NFL (8),
NFL Rookie of the Year (1957),
NFL MVP/Player of the Year (4),
Hall of Fame (1971)

Tackling Jimmy Brown was like running into an oak tree in the dark.

Sam Huff

*Hall of Fame linebacker,
New York Giants/Washington
Redskins*

The guy was so far ahead of his time. I always say that the Good Lord said, "I'm only going to do this once, and I'm not ever going to do it again." I don't take anything from Walter Payton and Emmitt Smith and O. J. or Barry Sanders—any of the great runners, but believe me, none compare to this guy. None.

John Wooten

He was the second-best athlete I've ever seen, behind Secretariat.

Gib Shanley

LEROY KELLY
Running Back (1964–73)
Pro Bowls (6), All-Pro (5),
Hall of Fame (1994)

Relegated to special teams work and status as one of the NFL's elite return men in 1964 and '65, Leroy Kelly was asked to replace an eight-time rushing champion and the game's most renowned player when Jim Brown suddenly retired before the 1966 season. Kelly stepped in and posted three straight, 1,000-yard seasons, while winning two rushing titles of his own and scoring a three-year total of 42 touchdowns.

Ron Smith

Leroy had the fastest start I've ever seen in my life. Officials used to call backfield in motion, and finally the Browns sent a film to league headquarters telling them to just watch this guy. He was so quick on that first step.

Gib Shanley

LEN FORD
Defensive End (1950–57)
Pro Bowls (4), All-NFL (5),
Hall of Fame (1976)

He was a fierce player and something to behold when he uncoiled and went after a passer.

Paul Brown

on defensive giant Len Ford

Len Ford played havoc with his outside rush and used his speed from sideline to sideline. From 1950–57, only Baltimore's Gino Marchetti could challenge his defensive end prowess.

Ron Smith

MICHAEL DEAN PERRY
Defensive Tackle (1988–94)
Pro Bowls (5), All-Pro (4)

From the start, many NFL insiders thought that Michael Dean Perry was a much larger talent, if not a much larger body, than his big brother William "The Refrigerator" Perry.

Jim Campbell
author

He was the most dominating interior lineman the Browns ever had since Jerry Sherk.

Russell Schneider
author/sportswriter

JERRY SHERK
Defensive Tackle (1970–81)
Pro Bowls (4), All-Pro (1)

The opinion was unanimous, beginning with Blanton Collier and continuing through every coaching regime thereafter: Nick Skorich, Forrest Gregg, and Sam Rutigliano. Without a doubt, Jerry Sherk was the best defensive lineman in the history of the Browns.

Russell Schneider

BILL GLASS
Defensive End (1962–68)
Pro Bowls (4)

Picture Billy Graham as a 6–5, 255-pound defensive end who could run over an offensive tackle and knock a quarterback on his can. Or as *Cleveland Press* columnist Frank Gibbons once wrote, "Everybody knows he is just as hard as the water from an old ranch well." That was Bill Glass: Preacher. Pass rusher.

Terry Pluto

CLAY MATTHEWS
Linebacker (1978–93)
Pro Bowls (4), All-Pro (3)

He was one of the greatest players to play the game. When I came to Cleveland, I remember some people said he would never play, that he wasn't tough enough, that he was a great athlete but not a football player. Boy, nothing could have been further from the truth. He had a standard of performance that was excellent, and he did it for an extended period of time. That's the portrait of greatness. He's one of the top three or four guys I ever had the privilege of coaching.

Marty Schottenheimer
on Clay Matthews

BILL WILLIS
Middle Guard/Middle Linebacker
(1946–53)
Pro Bowls (3), All-AAFC (3), All-NFL (4),
Hall of Fame (1977)

It was his quickness that helped him become a Hall of Famer. At 214 pounds, Bill Willis had to be quicker. The Browns boasted in their media guide that when Willis shot out of his crouch, he was moving at seventy miles per hour.

John Keim

I like to make contact with the opposing quarterback, just to let him know I am in the game.

Bill Willis

MARION MOTLEY
Fullback/Linebacker (1946–53)
Pro Bowls (1), All-AAFC (3), All-NFL (1),
Hall of Fame (1968)

Strangely enough, the Browns' most devastating runner could have been their most devastating tackler, too: Marion Motley. Early in his career, he remained a part of the team's goal line defense. It was his skill at linebacking and fullbacking that led author Paul Zimmerman to proclaim that Motley was "the greatest player" in the history of the NFL.

Jim Campbell

I've always believed that Motley could have gone into the Hall of Fame solely as a linebacker, if we had used him only at that position. He was as good as our great ones.

Paul Brown

He was pretty big and pretty bad.

Frank Gatski
Hall of Fame center (1946–56), on Motley

WARREN LAHR
Cornerback (1949–59)
All-NFL (1)

Lahr became one of the great defensive backs in the NFL, thanks to an auto accident that broke his arm and eliminated him as a quarterback candidate.

Russell Schneider

Lahr, a quarterback in college, initially tried out for that position in 1948, a slot already more than capably manned by the great Otto Graham. Lahr's accident, which took place during training camp, eliminated him from contending for any slot that year, but he returned in '49 as a defensive back, making the team and eventually recording 44 career interceptions, second all-time in Browns annals.

THOM DARDEN
Free Safety (1972–74, 1976–81)
Pro Bowls (1), All-Pro (1)

He was a consummate free safety. He could play center field like Duke Snider or Willie Mays. He made the big plays, the big tackle.

Sam Rutigliano
on Darden

CLARENCE SCOTT
Strong Safety (1971–83)
Pro Bowls (1), All-Pro (1)

Clarence Scott moved from cornerback to strong safety to free safety, but the important thing is that for more than a decade, he played at a level that allowed him to remain in the starting lineup longer than any defensive back in Browns history.

Jim Campbell

FRANK MINNIFIELD
Cornerback (1984–92)
Pro Bowls (4), All-Pro (4)

The 5–9 Minnifield loved jabbering with receivers, whom he once called the "scoundrels of the earth." He was fast and athletic—his vertical leap of 44 inches earned him the nickname "Sky," and he ran the 40-yard dash at 4.4 seconds.

John Keim

HORACE GILLOM
Punter (1947–56)
Pro Bowls (1)

Horace Gillom brought a different style of punting to the game. He was the first to kick for height and distance. His 80- and 75-yard punts are still in the Browns' record book. Gillom was a proponent of "hang time" long before the term gained widespread usage.

Jim Campbell

He was the best punter that ever put a toe to the pigskin. Man, did he punt!

Tommy James

Lou "The Toe" Groza
Kicker (1946–59, 1961–67)
Pro Bowls (9), All-NFL (6),
NFL Co-Player of the Year (1954),
Hall of Fame (1974)

Lou Groza was the best of the olden-days kickers. He kicked better under pressure than anyone I know. I can't remember him missing a clutch field goal.

Ben Agajanian

placekicker for 10 professional teams in three leagues over a 20-year period

He was always a great potential weapon when we were inside an opponent's 49-yard line. I know that Lou won more games in clutch situations with his kicking than any player in the game's history.

Paul Brown

ERIC METCALF
Punt Returner (1989–94)
Pro Bowls (2), All-Pro (1)

In 1993 he became the first player in NFL history to return two punts 75 yards or longer for touchdowns in the same game, when he set a club record with 166 yards against the Pittsburgh Steelers.

Beau Riffenburgh
author/journalist

A 190-pound "lightning bolt in a bottle."

Jim Campbell
on Eric Metcalf

BOBBY MITCHELL
Kick Returner (1958–61)
Pro Bowls (1), Hall of Fame (1983)

He was pro football's ultimate weapon, a dangerous running back, pass-catching wizard, and dazzling return man over 11 electrifying seasons. Nobody personified "big play potential" more than Bobby Mitchell.

Ron Smith

In his brief Cleveland career, Bobby Mitchell gained 5,916 combined yards and scored 38 touchdowns. He averaged 11.2 yards per punt return and 25.0 yards per kick return and scored three touchdowns in both categories. He averaged 5.4 yards—higher than Jim Brown—on 423 carries.

John Keim

PAUL BROWN

Head Coach (1946–62)

AAFC championships (4),
NFL championships (3),
Hall of Fame (1967)

Paul Brown has never gotten the credit he deserves. Vince Lombardi would come to our camp and watch practice. He learned from Paul, no question. Paul changed football a lot more than anyone ever thought of doing.

Otto Graham

He was like Red Auerbach to the NBA, Branch Rickey to baseball. Paul Brown was a giant.

Sam Rutigliano

All-America Football Conference MVPs

1947   **OTTO GRAHAM**

1948   **OTTO GRAHAM**
(co-MVP with Frankie Albert)

NFL MVPs

1951   **OTTO GRAHAM**

1953   **OTTO GRAHAM**

1955   **OTTO GRAHAM**

1957   **JIM BROWN**

1958   **JIM BROWN**

1963   **JIM BROWN**
(co-MVP with Y. A. Tittle)

1965   **JIM BROWN**

1968   **LEROY KELLY**
(co-MVP with Earl Morrall)

1980   **BRIAN SIPE**

Retired Browns Numbers

14 OTTO GRAHAM, *quarterback (1946–55)*

32 JIM BROWN, *running back (1957–65)*

45 ERNIE DAVIS, *running back*
(No. 1 overall pick who died of leukemia
before ever playing a game with the Browns,
May 18, 1963)

46 DON FLEMING, *defensive back (1960–62)*
(electrocuted on a construction project
in Florida in the spring of 1963)

76 LOU GROZA, *tackle/kicker (1946–59,
1961–67)*

NFL Rookies of the Year

1957 JIM BROWN
1958 BOBBY MITCHELL
(co-Rookie of the Year
with Jimmy Orr)

Defensive Rookie of the Year

1982 CHIP BANKS

Significant Browns Records

Scoring (career)	LOU GROZA	1,608 pts
Rushing (career)	JIM BROWN	12,312 yds
Passing (career)	BRIAN SIPE	23,713 yds
Passing TDs (career)	OTTO GRAHAM	174
Receptions (career)	OZZIE NEWSOME	662
Receiving (career)	OZZIE NEWSOME	7,980 yds
Receiving TDs (career)	GARY COLLINS	70
Passing TDs (game)	OTTO GRAHAM 10/14/49 vs. L.A. Dons	6
Rushing (game)	JIM BROWN 11/24/57 vs. L.A. Rams; 11/19/61 vs. Eagles	237 yds
Receiving (game)	MAC SPEEDIE 11/20/49 vs. Brooklyn Dodgers	228 yds
Interceptions (career)	THOM DARDEN	45
Kickoff return TDs	BOBBY MITCHELL	3
Punt return TDs	ERIC METCALF	5
Longest punt	HORACE GILLOM (11/28/54 vs. N.Y. Giants)	80 yds
Longest field goal	STEVE COX (10/21/84 vs. Bengals)	60 yds
Most TDs (career)	JIM BROWN	126

THE GREAT BROWNS TEAMS

YOU ARE THE GREATEST team ever to play football.

Bert Bell

NFL commissioner,
to the 1950 Cleveland Browns
in their locker room following
the Browns' 30–28 championship
game victory over the Los Angeles
Rams. Eleven future Hall of
Famers played in the contest

The Browns became the first professional team to ride through a season unbeaten. Not only had they won all 14 [regular-season] games, but they had streaked through 24 games without a loss, with 18 of them consecutive victories. Then they added another notch by burying the Buffalo Bills 49–7 [in the AAFC title game], and Brown rightfully called the Browns a "team with no weakness, the best I've ever coached." It was the last perfect record for a pro team until the 1972 Miami Dolphins.

Jack Clary

on the 1948 Cleveland Browns, in the All-America Football Conference

We were too good, if that sounds possible. Even in Cleveland the fans stopped coming because they just assumed we'd go out and dominate the opposition so strongly there would be no contest.

Paul Brown

on the 1948 Browns

We had Otto Graham, we had Motley, we had the guy I think was the greatest end who ever lived—Mac Speedie. George Young was probably the best defensive end I ever saw. We beat the hell out of them.

Tony Adamle

on the 1950 NFL champion Browns

There had been too much talk about our being the greatest team of all time.

Paul Brown

on the 1953 Browns, who nearly registered a perfect regular season record, before losing to Philadelphia in the finale. Cleveland had already clinched the division crown and viewed the Eagles game more as an anti-climatic warm-up for the title contest against Detroit

This is the finest team I've coached on a given day.

Paul Brown

on his 1954 Browns who had just swamped the Detroit Lions, 56–10, in the NFL title game

We had the greatest, most overachieving team in the history of football. That was what football was like in Cleveland in 1964. It was a group of guys who never cheated the fans or each other. And the fans, they were there for us every week—all 80,000 of them. I'll never forget the cheering.

Jim Brown

We weren't viewed as a very physical team, but we won because we had skilled players.

Paul Warfield

on the 1964 Browns

They had the greatest running back in the history of football, and a coach who wore a hearing aid. Their quarterback had a Ph.D. in math. They had a defensive end who was a preacher, and a halfback who became a millionaire.

Terry Pluto

on the 1964 world champion Cleveland Browns

The coach with the hearing aid is Blanton Collier; the QB with the doctorate is Frank Ryan; defensive end/preacher Bill Glass directs his ministering to prison inmates; and millionaire halfback Ernie Green, through his Ernie Green Industries, produces auto parts.

Other teams were better that decade [1960s], the players said. Some said the '65 team was better, others pointed to '68.

John Keim

Along came the Kardiac Kids in 1979–80, earning their nickname through a penchant for close games. During those two seasons, 26 of the Browns' 33 games were decided by a touchdown or less. The Browns won 16 of those games, including a 27–24 win in 1980 at Cincinnati that gave them their first division title since 1971, ending the worst drought in franchise history.

John Keim

We went from Pete Franklin having funeral services for us on his radio show to being the toast of the town.

Doug Dieken
during the Kardiac Kids era, 1979–80

That 1980 team was really talented offensively. We had the two Pruitts [Greg and Mike, both running backs], Calvin Hill—he could catch the ball—and Cleo Miller backed them up. At receiver, we had Reggie Rucker, Dave Logan, Ozzie Newsome, Ricky Feacher. Our quarterback, Brian Sipe, was MVP that year. Halfway through the season I said, "Brian, you're going to be the MVP of this league."

Joe DeLamielleure
Hall of Fame guard (1980–84)

Y ou can have a great team and the team may not get along. And there's so much turnover. A lot of times you don't have the closeness that we had that 1986 season. I can genuinely say that, without a doubt, that was the funnest and most rewarding team I played on.

Clay Matthews

11

OLD MUNICIPAL STADIUM

MY MEMORY OF THE stadium is that we're always playing in the snow or rain. On one side of the field, there is a shovel just stuck in the ground. On the other side, there's a tractor with one of its wheels off. There's a couple of buckets overturned and some huge tarps rolled up. It was like going to work in a factory; Cleveland was that kind of town back then.

Paul Wiggin

Cleveland Municipal Stadium

Photo Courtesy of the Cleveland Browns

I loved Cleveland Stadium. It was history. It was huge.

Jerry Sherk

The locker rooms weren't luxurious, but that didn't matter. They contained memories that provided everyone a sense of history. I remember seeing pictures from the 1950 championship team and seeing Groza and those guys against the lockers, and it gave you a sense of the people who were in those lockers before you. That became part and parcel of being with the Browns. There was an unspoken sense of greatness about that locker room.

Jerry Sherk

Chipped concrete greeted customers walking through a concourse as gray as a February day. Pillars blocked views for thousands of fans, who craned their necks to catch the action. Bleacher fans had a clear shot—but beware of the splinters in the aging, weather-pounded end zone seats. Forget about fresh paint, unless of course the dirt field needed another coat. And Lake Erie's biting winter winds left noses red and teeth chattering. Then there were the bathrooms. No urinal available? Try the sink. Everyone else did.

John Keim

It was big, it was cold, but it got noisy. The people of Cleveland were just fantastic, blue collar all the way. I enjoyed every bit of it.

Walt Michaels

on Municipal Stadium

Though only the bleachers were close to the field, they could be intimidating. Just ask any teams that had to deal with the Milk-Bone-throwing crowd of the Dawg Pound of the 1980s and '90s.

John Keim

When you walked into Cleveland Stadium, people right away felt they were going up against something awesome.

Bobby Mitchell

If there is a vision that I could recall from the stadium, it would be a game sometime in the fourth quarter where the game had started at one, but they would have to turn the lights on by the end. And there would be a light rain with a little wind, and it would be just perfect.

Clay Matthews

Twice during the 1980s, officials had teams switch directions to avoid the hurled debris from the Dawg Pound.

John Keim

It was where football really was football. Grass, mud, cold.

Dante Lavelli

As you got closer, you'd come up out of the dugout, go up four or five steps and, once you're up, you come onto the field and there would be a tremendous roar. That was one of the greatest experiences I had in athletics. Those fans would make me feel very, very enthusiastic, and all the adrenaline was flowing in every part of my body. It was a great old facility to play in.

Paul Warfield

Cleveland Stadium was like Yankee Stadium for nostalgia.

Dick Modzelewski

There was nothing that will compare to that walk down the tunnel. It's a time to collect your thoughts, and you can't feel the crowd until you get to that dugout step and then, Boom!, it's like someone turned the TV set on full blast.

Doug Dieken

Sometimes it would feel as if the sound just penetrated you, almost to the point where you could swear that you felt it in the ground if you just stood still. It was so loud, like being in a thunderstorm or in a wind tunnel. It was overwhelming.

Jerry Sherk

on the crowds at Cleveland Municipal Stadium

At halftime, I joined the crush of mankind waiting to go in the restroom. We were bunched so close together in that line that you could only see the person in front of you. Imagine my surprise when I finally got to the front of the line and found out there was no urinal, just a wall. I was sure glad I had my boots on.

Rick Patterson

fan

The first game we played there, I came out on the field and just felt like a midget.

Lou Groza

The fans had witnessed the best football had to offer for nearly 20 years under Paul Brown. They had seen in person one of the greatest quarterbacks ever in Otto Graham. They had watched the NFL's greatest running back in Jim Brown. Fourteen Hall of Famers called the stadium home. "Here we go Brownies, here we go!" will linger in their ears. That's why they kept coming back, drawn by the ghosts. That's why they braved all sorts of weather. That's why the stadium's dismantling brought tears to many.

John Keim

It was what football was all about. It was a just a classic stadium.

Don Strock
quarterback (1988)

RIVALRIES

BROWNS RIVALS HAVE INCLUDED the New York Yankees and San Francisco 49ers during the All-America Conference years; the Los Angeles Rams and Detroit Lions in the 1950–57 playoff era; the Pittsburgh Steelers from the '50s through the '90s; the Dallas Cowboys in the '60s; and, beginning with the AFL-NFL realignment of 1970, the Cincinnati Bengals and Houston Oilers. Then, of course, in the late '80s there were the dreaded Denver Broncos.

Jim Campbell

T hat was a great rivalry.

Dante Lavelli

*on the classic Cleveland–
San Francisco 49ers series that
began in the old All-America
Football Conference in 1946 and
continued on for several years
after both clubs joined the NFL
in 1950. The rivalry was at its
peak in the AAFC days. Of the
Browns four total losses in four
years, two were to the 49ers.
In the league's last year, 1949,
the two battled in the title game,
with the Browns prevailing, 21–7.
In Cleveland, 82,769 showed up
for the 1948 49ers game, estab-
lishing a Municipal Stadium
attendance mark that lasted
12 years*

I was intrigued and not ashamed to say so. I wondered, just as everyone else, what would happen. We knew everybody would be after us because that was the natural feeling of a rivalry.

Paul Brown

on the eve of the legendary 1950 season opener against the Philadelphia Eagles, Cleveland's first game as a new entrant into the NFL after four years of complete domination of the All-America Football Conference. The Browns humiliated the two-time defending NFL champions that Sept. 16 night, 35–10

The Giants provided the Browns their first great National Football League rivalry, as both were perennial playoff contenders into the mid 1960s.

Jim Campbell

The Giants were a team that had driven Paul Brown to distraction. They were a team that knew how to beat the Cleveland Browns, even on the Giants' worst day.

Terry Pluto

since the Browns' entry into the NFL in 1950, the Giants had held a certain sway over Cleveland, often sweeping regular-season series during the Browns' dynasty years and always ensuring that Cleveland victories came hard-earned

If Y. A. Tittle can beat the Browns, we'll vote him a share of the championship money.

Joe Robb

St. Louis Cardinals defensive end, urging the lowly New York Giants to upset Cleveland in the 1964 regular-season finale. A Giants win would have enabled the Cardinals rather than Browns to advance to the NFL Championship Game against Baltimore. As it was, the Browns annihilated New York, 52–20

Pessimism stalked the Browns as the 1954 championship game approached. They had not beaten Detroit since 1950. People were beginning to wonder if Paul Brown would ever defeat a team coached by Buddy Parker.

Jack Clary

After losing seven of nine contests to the Lions (including preseason) upon entering the NFL in 1950, Cleveland trounced Detroit in the '54 title game, 56–10.

Buddy Parker was about the only coach to get the best of Paul Brown in head-to-head competition. It must have been particularly galling to Brown since Parker's use of football's renegades was the opposite of Brown's emphasis on players with character.

Jim Campbell

Starting in 1950, the Pittsburgh Steelers became a natural rival, located some 120 miles from Cleveland. Art Modell recognized the importance of the rivalry with Pittsburgh and twice insisted the Steelers and Browns be in the same division, during NFL realignment for 1967 and 1970.

Morris Eckhouse
author

For the people of Cleveland, when you beat Pittsburgh, it was almost like, "Screw the rest of the season." You can make or break your season just by beating them.

Doug Dieken

You could really feel the crowd, and most players fed off that. Against Pittsburgh, there was a constant roar, even in between plays. That fills your body so full of adrenaline, and it gives you that extra effort. When that roar happens and you're running on a play, if you couldn't get to the ball carrier, you'd peel back and just drill somebody, even a lineman.

Jerry Sherk

The fans came on the field as if we had won a world championship. They were pulling on the goalposts. You've got people patting you on the helmet. I was panicking. If it was one, or two, or three hundred, fine. But it was thousands.

Greg Pruitt

after scoring two touchdowns in a 21–16 victory over the Steelers his rookie season of 1973

I kept my mouth shut and my helmet on when I went to Pittsburgh.

Joe "Turkey" Jones

defensive end (1970–71, 1973, 1975–78)

The townspeople identified with it more than any other game, so when we played Pittsburgh, it was an unbelievable week. You could sense the mood of the town before and after the game. If we won the game, the town would be on fire and people would go to work for a couple weeks in a positive mood. And if we lost the game, it would be the exact opposite.

Jerry Sherk
on the Pittsburgh rivalry

It was like a playoff game. You don't want to think you cranked it up to a higher level, but you did. There was a lot of pride and honor on the line. And it was always physical. We got Jack Lambert thrown out of two or three games, which was probably the best part of our game plan.

Doug Dieken

on the Pittsburgh Steelers rivalry

The Pittsburgh rivalry's most memorable game in recent years occurred in Cleveland Stadium on Oct. 24, 1993, when Eric Metcalf nearly beat the Steelers single-handedly. On that day, Metcalf equaled a National Football League record for punt returns for touchdowns in one game with two.

Jim Campbell

We can expect a typical Browns-Bengals game.

Otto Graham

before the very first game between the two, in the 1970 preseason

The points came so fast that it seemed a recount might be needed to determine who won Ohio's bragging rights.

Joe Kay

Associated Press, on the second-highest scoring game in league history— Cincinnati's 58–48 victory over the Browns in 2004—behind only the Washington Redskins' 72–41 win over the New York Giants, Nov. 27, 1966. The Bengals and Browns combined for 49 first downs and 966 total yards

Kelly Holcomb threw for 400 yards and five touchdowns—and lost.

Joe Kay

on the Browns' 58–48 loss to intrastate rival Cincinnati, Nov. 28, 2004, at Paul Brown Stadium—the second-highest-scoring game in NFL history. Holcomb completed 30 of 39 passing attempts for 413 yards, five TDs, and two interceptions

In the 1987 AFC title rematch in Denver, Elway and Co. prevailed again, 38–33. This game would be remembered for "The Fumble."

Jim Campbell

The Browns, down 38–31 late in the fourth quarter, were driving for the tying touchdown, when running back Earnest Byner fumbled on the Denver 2-yard line.

A POUND
OF BROWNS FANS
(AND OTHER DEVOTEES)

It was like Mardi Gras at a football game. The Dawg Pound reminded me of the inner city. It was like the rest of the stadium was the county and the Dawg Pound was the inner city where the rowhouses are and where they had gang-infested areas. We didn't have to worry about people coming in from other towns and displaying their team logos and colors in the Dawg Pound.

Michael Jackson (Dyson)
wide receiver (1991–95)

We call our section the original Dawg Pound. The guys in the front row brought in a dog house. One of the guys painted his face half orange and half brown. And we were the first ones to start barking.

Vince Erwin
longtime Dawg Pounder

When they'd introduce the players and you'd come out of the dugout, the fans would cheer so hard that the ground just shook. Just talking about it gives me goose pimples. I have spent my life in pro football, and there was nothing like the roar of those fans and that old Stadium rattling.

John Wooten

I never played in another stadium where you could just walk out of the dressing room down that long tunnel to the field and just feel the drama. It was a long, dark, damp tunnel. At the end, you could see the light. You heard the fans, and they grew louder with every step. When you reached the light and ran onto the field, it wasn't just applause. It was thunder. It made your blood pump, your heart pound. You felt as if you had just gone to football heaven.

Paul Warfield

The worse the weather was, the more fondness the fans had for it.

Jerry Sherk

You just wanted to pound as many beers as possible, but before you had a chance to do it, people kept walking over and saying, "Thanks for a great season." I was like, "Hey, we let you down today." But that's what makes football in Cleveland so great: the fans.

Doug Dieken

after the heart-breaking playoff loss to the Oakland Raiders in 1980, ending the Kardiac Kids' improbable run

The fact that we were winning came from the fact that we had a good following. It's always nice to play under those conditions where there's fan satisfaction.

Lou Groza

When I think about Cleveland, I think of the strong character the people have there, the loyalty for their families and the loyalty they have for their sports teams.

Jerry Sherk

I live and die with the Browns every year.

Hank Aaron

baseball immortal

It seems like they breed little Browns babies there. You had to be a Cleveland Browns fan. When I went back a couple years ago, it was an eye-opener. I didn't understand the magnitude when I was playing. But there are some die-hard fans, and that's their entertainment. They believe in their Brownies.

Joe "Turkey" Jones

It was almost like the fans expected a certain kind of play from you and they wouldn't take anything less. They couldn't fire you or trade you, but they could sure let you know how they felt about it.

Greg Pruitt

Our fans identified with Cleveland Stadium. They were proud to sit in those seats for 30 years, and their parents had sat in them before they did.

Ozzie Newsome

You'd see the same faces when you walked out of that dugout. Young kids and older people that were there every Sunday. I remember one guy named Buddy, an older guy, who would always say, "Hey! Big Jim!" After seven or eight years, you got to know these people.

Jim Kanicki

What I remember most is that it was filled with really good, rabid, smart fans, who came whether we were winning or losing, whether it was hot or cold, dry or snowy.

Dale Lindsey

The back of our seats had slots where the cold wind blew at our backs. The wind seemed to increase the aroma of the hot dogs and hot chocolate all around us.

Phyllis Mesko
fan,
on her top-row upper-deck seats
at Municipal Stadium

This [1986] had become the year of the Dawg, the nickname bestowed on the Browns defense by Frank Minnifield and fellow corner Hanford Dixon the year before. Cleveland embraced the moniker, and the bleachers evolved into the Dawg Pound. Fans, some wearing dog masks and waving bones, barked at players who woofed right back. Milk-Bones became a pre-game snack.

John Keim

Our relationship with our fans really made our team special, and it created a bond with the fans and with each other.

Frank Minnifield

We heard Hanford Dixon sort of grunting at people out on the field. Then he got closer and we realized he wasn't grunting, he was barking. Then we saw it on television on one of the highlights, and that's all it took for us to get going.

Vince Erwin

It was at practice. I was trying to get the defensive linemen going, to get a rush on the quarterback. I was thinking the quarterback is the cat and the defensive line is the dogs.

Hanford Dixon
in 1985

Little did the Browns' starting corner-backs know that their woofing would be the start of quite possibly the largest, loudest, longest-running canine commotion this side of *101 Dalmatians.*

Roger Gordon
author

A Saturday afternoon, a couple of beers, a costume shop, a dog mask, and you've got it.

John "Big Dawg" Thompson
the Pound's unofficial
"ambassador of bone,"
on how he became "impounded"

Brown-and-orange hair shirts should be officially licensed NFL merchandise because you remember Pat Summerall's 49-yard field goal through the snow in the last game of the 1958 season in Yankee Stadium. You remember "Red Right 88." You remember "The Drive" and "The Fumble" and "I had no choice." Your heart has been in the shop more times than a '46 Chevy.

Dan Coughlin
former Plain Dealer *writer*

They're a meat-and-potatoes team from the old era of pro football. They're a blue-collar team in a blue-collar town.

Vince Erwin

THE
LOCKER ROOM

THAT CHECK WAS FOR a little over $8,000. I made a photocopy of it before I cashed it. I figured I'd never see a check that big again. I used some of it to buy a Hammond organ. I had played the piano a little bit as a kid, and I was in the band in high school. I always wanted an organ.

Monte Clark

*on his player's share earned
from beating the Baltimore Colts
in the 1964 world championship
game*

A week after Paul Brown was fired, Blanton Collier was hired as only the second coach in the 17-year history of the Cleveland Browns. He signed a three-year contract worth $35,000 annually—less than half the $82,500 Paul Brown was being paid not to coach the Browns.

Terry Pluto

If I were the Browns' coach, I would tell the fullback that I would trade him if he didn't block and fake. The Browns will not win anything as long as Jim Brown is there.

Otto Graham

Don Paul was really a character. One of the things he would do before practice on rainy days was to "hit a home run." He'd stand where home plate was on the infield part of Cleveland Stadium, knock an imaginary ball over the wall and then slide into each base as he shouted the play-by-play. He'd be covered with mud before we even started practice. It really cracked up the players, but I don't think Paul Brown appreciated it that much.

Dick Gallagher

assistant coach (1947–49, 1955–59),
on the Browns' three-time
Pro Bowl cornerback, who
played from 1954 through 1958

What I remember most about playing for the Browns was the player introductions. You'd run down that dark tunnel and see the light at the end of it. As we came out and up the dugout steps, those 80,000 fans would roar. I mean, roar. They shook that old stadium. I feel very lucky to have heard those kinds of cheers. Few people do.

Paul Warfield

The most reckless football player I've ever seen.

Paul Brown

on fullback Harry "Chick" Jagade (1951–53)

You'll never believe this, but within four hours after a game, I'd drink a case of beer and then a case of pop, trying to put back on the weight I'd lost. White Castle hamburgers. There were eight to a box of those little hamburgers. I'd order six boxes and eat 48 of them in a sitting.

Dick Schafrath

I was a garbage machine. I was in every all-you-can-eat contest all over the state. At one place, I ate 24 lobster tails and 15 halves of chicken. In one sitting.

Dick Schafrath

Paul Brown never allows us to drink water on the field. I firmly believe that if you go out on a hot day and gulp down some cold water, it's just like adding 40 years to your age. You become lazy and groggy, and it's an effort to move.

Otto Graham

in 1952

All the rituals before the game, starting with the nervous energy at the hotel during breakfast. Doug Dieken drinking his 13 cups of coffee. The tingle in your stomach as you took a cab to the stadium.

Jerry Sherk

on pre-game rites

No more Red Right 88.

Sign hanging in Cleveland Stadium

during the Browns–Jets 1986 divisional playoff game, won in double overtime by the Browns, 23–20. The sign was in reference to the final play of Cleveland's last playoff game six seasons earlier, in1980, when quarterback Brian Sipe threw a game-ending end-zone interception, killing the Browns' last hopes in a 14–12 playoff loss to Oakland

It's my ballgame. I'm going to run my ballgame. I'm the owner, coach, president, general manager, and trainer.

Art Modell

In 10 years of taking the ball from him, frankly, I don't remember him saying a word on the field.

Otto Graham

on center Frank Gatski

He is the strongest man in football and also the biggest. When he rushes the passer with those oak-tree arms of his way up in the air, he's 12 feet tall. And if he gets to you, the whole world suddenly starts spinning.

Fran Tarkenton

Minnesota Vikings Hall of Fame quarterback,
on defensive end Doug Atkins,
Cleveland's No. 1 draft choice in 1953, who later became a Hall of Famer with the Chicago Bears

He was a Flea all right, but with the toughness of a roach.

Terry Pluto
on 5–10, 170-pound punt/kick returner Walter "Flea" Roberts

Paul Brown once had been asked, "How'd you like to have that Doc Blanchard?" And he replied: "The man I've got in mind is called Marion Motley, and he's better than Blanchard."

Sport Magazine
November 1952

I tell my brother I wouldn't give him a break on the field. I wouldn't give him a break or anybody else. If they can't take it, they shouldn't be out there. I'm going to do my job.

Len Ford

All of life is mastering the fundamentals. . . . Truth is where the toe meets the ball.

Lou Groza

15

BROWNS WORLD CHAMPIONSHIP ROSTERS

No team in the history of professional football began its legacy with a better championship record than the Cleveland Browns, sweeping all four years of its reign in the All-America Football Conference, before picking off the NFL with three more championship titles in its first six years in the senior circuit. They added an eighth crown in 1964 but have drunk from defeat's bitter cup ever since, losing three league and three conference championship games over the past 40 years.

1946

13–2

(includes 14–9 AAFC Championship Game
win over New York Yankees)

Paul Brown, *head coach*

Adams, Chet	**DT**	Kolesar, Bob	G
Akins, Al	HB-DB	**Lavelli, Dante**	**E**
Blandin, Ernie	**DT**	**Lewis, Cliff**	**DB**-QB
Cheroke, George	G	Lund, Bill	HB-DB
Colella, Tom	**DB-HB**	Maceau, Mel	C-LB
Coppage, Al	E	**Motley, Marion**	**FB-LB**
Daniell, Jim	**T**	Rokisky, John	E
Evans, Fred	HB-DB	**Rymkus, Lou**	**T**
Fekete, Gene	FB-LB	**Saban, Lou**	**LB**-FB
Gatski, Frank	C-LB	**Scarry, Mo**	**C-LB**
Graham, Otto	**QB**-DB	Schwenk, Bud	QB
Greenwood, Don	**HB-DB**	Smith, Gaylon	FB-LB
Groza, Lou	T-K	**Speedie, Mac**	**E**
Harrington, John	E	Steuber, Bob	HB-DB
Houston, Lin	**G**	Terrell, Ray	HB-DB
Jones, Edgar		**Ulinski, Ed**	**G**
"Special Delivery"	**HB**-DB	**Willis, Bill**	**MG**
Kapter, Alex	G	**Yonakor, John**	**DE**
		Young, George	**DE**

Starting lineups in bold

1947

13–1–1

(includes 14–3 AAFC Championship Game
win over New York Yankees)

Paul Brown, *head coach*

Adamle, Tony	FB-LB	**Lavelli, Dante**	**E**
Adams, Chet	**OT-DT**	**Lewis, Cliff**	**DB**-QB
Allen, Ermal	QB-DB	Lund, Bill	HB-DB
Blandin, Ernie	T	Maceau, Mel	C-LB
Boedeker, Bill	**HB**-DB	Mayne, Lew	HB-DB
Colella, Tom	**DB-HB**	**Motley, Marion**	**FB-LB**
Cowan, Bob	HB-DB	Piskor, Roman	T
Dellerba, Spiro	FB-LB	**Rymkus, Lou**	**T**
Dewar, Jim	HB-DB	**Saban, Lou**	**LB**
Gatski, Frank	C-LB	**Scarry, Mo**	**C-LB**
Gaudio, Bob	G-LB	Shurnas, Marshall	E
Gillom, Horace	E-P	**Simonetti, Len**	**DT**
Graham, Otto	**QB-DB**	**Speedie, Mac**	**E**
Greenwood, Don	**HB-DB**	Terrell, Ray	HB-DB
Groza, Lou	T-K	**Ulinski, Ed**	**G**
Houston, Lin	**G**	**Willis, Bill**	**MG**
Humble, Weldon	**LB**-G	**Yonakor, John**	**DE**
Jones, Edgar		**Young, George**	**DE**
"Special Delivery"	HB-DB		

1948

15–0

(includes 49–7 AAFC Championship Game
win over Buffalo Bills)

Paul Brown, *head coach*

Adamle, Tony	LB-FB		Kosikowski, Frank	DE
Adams, Chet	DT		**Lavelli, Dante**	E
Agase, Alex	G-LB		**Lewis, Cliff**	DB-QB
Boedeker, Bill	HB-DB		Maceau, Mel	C-LB
Cline, Ollie	FB-LB		**Motley, Marion**	FB-LB
Colella, Tom	DB-HB		Parseghian, Ara	HB-DB
Cowan, Bob	HB-DB		Pucci, Ben	T
Gatski, Frank	C		**Rymkus, Lou**	T
Gaudio, Bob	G-LB		**Saban, Lou**	LB
Gillom, Horace	E-P		Sensanbaugher, Dean	HB-DB
Graham, Otto	QB-DB		Simonetti, Len	T
Grigg, Chubby	DT		**Speedie, Mac**	E
Groza, Lou	T-K		Terlep, George	QB
Houston, Lin	G		**Ulinski, Ed**	G
Humble, Weldon	LB-G		**Willis, Bill**	MG
James, Tommy	DB-HB		**Yonakor, John**	DE
Jones, Dub	HB-DB		**Young, George**	DE
Jones, Edgar "Special Delivery"	HB			

1949

11–1–2

(includes 31–21 AAFC playoff win over Buffalo
Bills and 21–7 championship game victory
over San Francisco 49ers)

Paul Brown, *head coach*

Adamle, Tony	LB-FB		**Lavelli, Dante**	E
Agase, Alex	G-LB		**Lewis, Cliff**	DB-QB
Boedeker, Bill	HB		**Motley, Marion**	FB-LB
Gatski, Frank	C		O'Connor, Bill	DE
Gaudio, Bob	G-LB		**Palmer, Derrell**	DT
Gillom, Horace	E-P		Parseghian, Ara	HB
Graham, Otto	QB		**Rymkus, Lou**	T
Grigg, Chubby	DT		**Saban, Lou**	LB
Groza, Lou	T-K		**Speedie, Mac**	E
Horvath, Les	HB-DB		Spencer, Joe	T
Houston, Lin	G		Sustersic, Ed	FB-LB
Humble, Weldon	LB-G		Thompson, Tommy	C-LB
James, Tommy	DB-HB		**Ulinski, Ed**	G
Jones, Dub	HB		**Willis, Bill**	MG
Jones, Edgar "Special Delivery"	HB		**Yonakor, John**	DE
Lahr, Warren	DB-HB		**Young, George**	DE

1950

12–2

(includes 8–3 NFL American Conference playoff victory over New York Giants and 30–28 title game win over Los Angeles Rams)

Paul Brown, *head coach*

Adamle, Tony	LB-FB	**Jones, Dub**	HB
Agase, Alex	LB	**Kissell, John**	DT
Bumgardner, Rex	HB	**Lahr, Warren**	DB
Carpenter, Ken	HB	**Lavelli, Dante**	E
Cole, Emerson	FB	**Lewis, Cliff**	S-QB
Ford, Len	DE	Martin, Jim	T-DE
Gatski, Frank	C	Moselle, Dom	HB
Gibron, Abe	G	**Motley, Marion**	FB-LB
Gillom, Horace	E-P	Palmer, Derrell	DT
Gorgal, Ken	DB	Phelps, Don	DB-HB
Graham, Otto	QB	**Rymkus, Lou**	T
Grigg, Chubby	DT	Sandusky, John	DT
Groza, Lou	T-K	**Speedie, Mac**	E
Herring, Hal	LB-C	Thompson, Tommy	C-LB
Houston, Lin	G	**Willis, Bill**	MG
Humble, Weldon	LB-G	**Young, George**	DE
James, Tommy	DB-HB		

1954

10–3

(includes 56–10 NFL Championship Game
win over Detroit Lions)

Paul Brown, *head coach*

Adamle, Tony	LB		**James, Tommy**	DB-HB
Armstrong, Quincy	C		Jones, Dub	HB
Atkins, Doug	DE		King, Don	T
Bassett, Maurice	FB		**Kissell, John**	DT
Bradley, Harold	G		Konz, Ken	DB
Brewster, Darrel	E		**Lahr, Warren**	DB-HB
Catlin, Tom	LB-C		**Lavelli, Dante**	E
Colo, Don	DT		**Massey, Carlton**	DE
Ford, Len	DE		**McCormack, Mike**	MG
Forester, Herschel	G		**Michaels, Walt**	LB
Gain, Bob	T-G		Morrison, Fred	FB
Gatski, Frank	C		Noll, Chuck	G-LB
Gibron, Abe	G		**Paul, Don**	DB
Gillom, Horace	E-P		Ratterman, George	QB
Gorgal, Ken	DB		**Renfro, Ray**	HB
Graham, Otto	QB		**Reynolds, Billy**	HB
Groza, Lou	T-K		**Sandusky, John**	T
Hanulak, Chet	HB			

1955
10–2–1

(includes 38–14 NFL Championship Game
win over Los Angeles Rams)
Paul Brown, *head coach*

Bassett, Maurice	FB	**Lahr, Warren**	**DB**
Bradley, Harold	**G**	**Lavelli, Dante**	**E**
Brewster, Darrel	**E**	**Massey, Carlton**	**DE**
Colo, Don	**DT**	**McCormack, Mike**	**T**
Ford, Henry	HB	**Michaels, Walt**	**LB**
Ford, Len	**DE**	**Modzelewski, Ed**	**FB**
Forester, Herschel	G	**Morrison, Fred**	**HB**
Gain, Bob	**MG**	**Noll, Chuck**	**LB**
Gatski, Frank	**C**	Palumbo, Sam	C-LB
Gibron, Abe	**G**	**Paul, Don**	**DB**
Gillom, Horace	E-P	Perini, Pete	FB-LB
Graham, Otto	**QB**	Petitbon, Johnny	HB-DB
Groza, Lou	**T**-K	Ratterman, George	QB
James, Tommy	**DB**-HB	**Renfro, Ray**	**HB**
Jones, Tom	T	Sandusky, John	T
Jones, Dub	HB	Smith, Bob	HB
Kissell, John	**DT**	Weber, Chuck	G-DE-LB
Konz, Ken	**DB**	White, Bob	DB

1964

11–3–1

(includes 27–0 NFL Championship Game
win over Baltimore Colts)

Blanton Collier, *head coach*

Beach, Walter	**DB**	Kelly, Leroy	HB
Benz, Larry	**DB**	Lucci, Mike	LB
Bettridge, Ed	LB	McNeil, Clifton	FL
Brewer, Johnny	**TE**	Memmelaar, Dale	G
Brown, Jim	**FB**	**Modzelewski, Dick**	**DT**
Brown, John	**T**	**Morrow, John**	**C**
Bundra, Mike	DT	Ninowski, Jim	QB
Caylor, Lowell	DB	Parker, Frank	DT
Clark, Monte	T	**Parrish, Bernie**	**DB**
Collins, Gary	**FL**-P	Raimey, Dave	DB
Costello, Vince	**LB**	Roberts, Walter	FL-PR-KR
Fichtner, Ross	DB	**Ryan, Frank**	**QB**
Fiss, Galen	**LB**	Scales, Charlie	FB
Franklin, Bobby	**DB**	**Schafrath, Dick**	**T**
Gain, Bob	DT	Sczurek, Stan	LB
Glass, Bill	**DE**	Shoals, Roger	G-T
Green, Ernie	**HB**	**Warfield, Paul**	**WR**
Groza, Lou	K	**Wiggin, Paul**	**DE**
Hickerson, Gene	**G**	Williams, Sid	DE
Houston, Jim	**LB**	**Wooten, John**	**G**
Hutchinson, Tom	E		
Kanicki, Jim	**DT**		

BIBLIOGRAPHY

Bethea, Elvin. Personal interview. 11 March 2003.

Byrne, Steve and Jim Campbell, Mark Craig. *The Cleveland Browns: A 50-year Tradition*. Bob Moon, ed. Champaign, Ill.: Sagamore Publishing, 1995.

Carroll, Bob and Michael Gershman, et al. *Total Browns: The Official Encyclopedia of the Cleveland Browns*. Kingston, N.Y.: Total Sports and NFL Properties, 1999.

Clary, Jack. *Cleveland Browns*. New York: Macmillan Publishing Co., 1973.

Eckhouse, Morris. *Day by Day in Cleveland Browns History*. New York: Leisure Press, 1984.

Gordon, Roger. *Cleveland Browns A to Z*. Champaign, Ill.: Sports Publishing LLC, 2002.

Gordon, Roger. *Cleveland Browns Facts & Trivia*. Berlin, Wis.: Ravenstone Publishing Group, Inc., 1999.

Grabowski, John F. *Cleveland Browns Trivia*. Boston, Mass.: Quinlan Press, 1987.

Graham, Duey. *OttoMatic: The Remarkable Story of Otto Graham*. Wayne, Mich.: Immortal Investments Publishing, 2004.

Graham, Otto. *Otto Graham—"T" Quarterback*. New York: Prentice-Hall, Inc., 1953.

Graham, Otto. Personal interviews. 6 February 1995, 21 August 1995, 16 March 1999, 17 November 1995, 5 September 2000.

Graham, Tim, ed. *Back Home: The Rebirth of the Cleveland Browns, Vol. I*. Emeryville, Calif.: Woodford Press, 1999.

Graham, Tim, ed. *Back Home: The Rebirth of the Cleveland Browns, Vol. II*. Emeryville, Calif.: Woodford Press, 1999.

Groza, Lou with Mark Hodermarsky. *The Toe: The Lou Groza Story*. Dubuque, Iowa: Kendall/Hunt Publishing Co., 1996.

Heaton, Chuck. *The Cleveland Browns: Power and Glory*. Englewood Cliffs, N.J.: Prentice-Hall, Inc., 1974.

Hession, Joseph and Kevin Lynch. *War Stories from the Field*. San Francisco, Calif.: Foghorn Press, 1994.

Huler, Scott. *On Being Brown: What It Means to Be a Cleveland Browns Fan*. Cleveland, Ohio: Gray & Company, Publishers, 1999.

Italia, Bob. *The Cleveland Browns*. Edina, Minn.: Abdo & Daughters, 1996.

Kay, Joe. "Bengals top Browns in 58–48 surprise." *USA Today*, 29 November 2004: 7C.

Keim, John. *Legends by the Lake: The Cleveland Browns at Municipal Stadium*. Akron, Ohio: The University of Akron Press, 1999.

King, Peter. *Football: A History of the Professional Game*. New York: Time Inc. Home Entertainment, 1996.

Knight, Jonathan. *Kardiac Kids: The Story of the 1980 Cleveland Browns*. Kent, Ohio: The Kent State University Press, 2003.

Lavelli, Dante. Personal interview. 10 May 2004.

Levy, Bill. *Return to Glory: The Story of the Cleveland Browns*. Cleveland, Ohio: The World Publishing Company, 1965.

Levy, Bill. *Sam, Sipe, & Company: The Story of the Cleveland Browns*. Cleveland, Ohio: J. T. Zubal & P. D. Dole, Publishers, 1981.

Long, Tim. *Browns Memories*. Cleveland, Ohio: Gray & Company, Publishers, 1996.

Natali, Alan. *Brown's Town: 20 Famous Browns Talk Amongst Themselves*. Wilmington, Ohio: Orange Frazer Press, 2001.

Pluto, Terry. *When All the World Was Browns Town*. New York City: Simon & Schuster, 1997.

Poplar, Michael G. with James A. Toman. *Fumble! The Browns, Modell, and the Move: An Insider's Story*. Hinckley, Ohio: Cleveland Landmarks Press, Inc., 1997.

Ross, Alan. "Brownout." *Lindy's 1999 Pro Football*: 26.

Ross, Alan. "In Otto Words: Otto Graham Tribute." *Cleveland Browns 2004 Yearbook*: 170–171.

Ross, Alan. "Joe DeLamielleure: Human Highlight Reel." *Cleveland Browns 2003 Yearbook*: 150.

Ross, Alan. "No Brain, No Gain." *Sporting News Special Collectors' Edition: Pro Football's Tough Guys, 2003*: 71, 72.

Schneider, Russell. *The Best of the Cleveland Browns Memories*. Hinckley, Ohio: Moonlight Publishing, 1999.

Shmelter, Richard. *The Browns: Cleveland's Team*. Champaign, Ill.: Sports Publishing Inc., 1999.

Smith, Ron. *Pro Football's Heroes of the Hall*. St. Louis: The Sporting News, 2003.

Stewart, Todd, ed. *Cleveland Browns 2004 Media Guide*. Cleveland, Ohio: Cleveland Browns, 2004.

Wooten, John. Personal interview. 28 May 2003.

Young, James V. and Arthur F. McClure. *Remembering Their Glory: Sports Heroes of the 1940s*. South Brunswick, N.J.: A. S. Barnes and Company, 1977.

Zimmerman, Paul. *A Thinking Man's Guide to Pro Football, Revised Edition*. New York: E. P. Dutton & Co., 1971.

WEBSITES:

www.fanmonster.com/blogs/ace/index.asp?month=6 &year=2004&select_case=month

INDEX